Cold Water

Women and Girls of Lira, Uganda

Editors
Jody Lynn McBrien
Julia Gentleman Byers

FOUNTAIN PUBLISHERS
www.fountainpublishers.co.ug

Fountain Publishers
P.O. Box 488
Kampala
E-mail: sales@fountainpublishers.co.ug
publishing@fountainpublishers.co.ug
Website: www.fountainpublishers.co.ug

Distributed in Europe and Commonwealth countries outside Africa by:
African Books Collective Ltd,
P.O. Box 721,
Oxford OX1 9EN, UK.
Tel/Fax: +44(0) 1869 349110
E-mail: orders@africanbookscollective.com
Website: www.africanbookscollective.com

© Jody Lynn McBrien & Julia Gentleman Byers 2015
First published 2015

All rights reserved. No part of this publication may be reproduced, stored in a retrieval system or transmitted in any form or by any means electronic, mechanical, photocopying, recording or otherwise without the prior written permission of the publisher.

ISBN: 978-9970-25-885-7

Dedications

This book is a collaboration between women of Lira and women professors in the United States. As such, we are happy that two of our Ugandan colleagues chose to include dedications. We end with those of the editors:

Aceng Emma Okite: My dedication is to the women and girls of Lango sub-region, northern Uganda and all women in the world who stood with us during the two decades that northern Uganda was in turmoil at the hands of the Lord's Resistance Army led by Joseph Kony, who killed and abducted thousands of innocent children. May their souls rest in peace.

I am grateful to Jody and Julia who had a heart to come to Lira and the Lango sub-region to share our plight and help us recollect our broken pieces as we tried to recover. May the Almighty bless them abundantly!

I also dedicate this book to my only daughter, Alum Anne Mary, who saw women and children suffer in Internally Displaced Persons' camps. I pray she becomes a change-maker and a voice to the voiceless in the world. I do not forget my sons, Obong Gerald James, Oree Evans Sam, and Ogwal Andrea Noll.

Finally, I dedicate this book to my late father, John Baptist Otim, who inspired me and planted the seeds of girl children's education in our family, but never lived to see its fruits. May he rest in peace. To my dear mother Ayaa Lucy Atim, I say thank you; and that also goes to all my brothers as well as my sister. Always remember the vulnerable and the suffering people in the world.

Okwir Betty Regina: My dedication is to my beloved family, all Women Achievers, girls in Lira District as well as Lango sub-region, northern Uganda, and all women in the world that stood with us in prayers while we were torn apart at the hands of Lord's Resistance Army led by Joseph Kony.

We appreciate the dedication and effort of our dear friends Drs Jody McBrien and Julia Byers who came to Lira to share with us our sorrows and burdens when we were broken apart. This book is also dedicated to King Solomon Nursery and Primary School management, staff, and community for their support of school coordination in the community, and especially for girls and women around the school community.

I also sincerely thank Emma Aceng and Esther Atoo for introducing me to our friends Drs Jody McBrien and Julia Byers. Lastly, I thank my husband, Deputy Mayor Lira Municipal Council, Okwir Johnson Dengai, for his support towards this noble cause to produce this book for the benefit of girls and women in need of support.

Julia Byers: I am deeply indebted to my sons, Ernest and Liam Byers, and my daughter-to-be, Tiffany Warren, who were supportive of my going to Africa, Uganda in particular, knowing my desire to make the global world closer. They were the ones who greeted me at the airport and helped me transition back to American culture. It was a culture shock to return to the US and truly feel the abundance and wealth that many take for granted. The real wealth I found was in the resilience and stories of the women who shared in the maternal need to want the collective best for our children.

One of the gifts of my life is knowing that Steve, my companion and supporter, truly understands and deeply cares about the goals of this project. With his love and guidance, my hours away fuelled us in knowing the strength of what a community can do. My mother, Margaret Gentleman, a sage at 91 years old, and my brother Bob and his partner Bill, are forever close in my heart as we bridge cultures and continue to learn about life.

I would also like to acknowledge graduate students in art therapy at Lesley University, especially Amy Huffaker. From the moment of hearing about the trips to Uganda, Amy tirelessly offered her support to give a public voice to the women of Lira. With compassion and fortitude, Amy became a true companion from many miles away in her steadfastness to make this collection of authors viable and strong.

Mostly, it is the women of Lira that totally inspire me. I want to extend my immense gratitude for their generosity and kindness in welcoming us into their lives. I will always be inspired by their work and lives. The gift of lifelong friendship is a treasure that exceeds everything. Thank you!

Jody McBrien: I dedicate this book to my family. First, to my children, Brendan and Kathleen, and my son-in law, Bryan. My deepest love to you all. Throughout our lives together, you have taught me so much. You have been my inspiration for living. I also thank my parents, who have honoured and respected my path, although it differed from their own. And, of course, I dedicate this book to my husband, Richard Stammer. Over so many months, I have said "No" to you about various social gatherings and events as I needed to complete the manuscript. As you accompanied me to Uganda in 2013, I know you came to understand the beauty of the country and the people I have come to love. Thank you for your fortitude, my love!

Finally, this book is dedicated to the women and children of northern Uganda, many of whom lost their lives in the terrible war with Joseph Kony and the Lord's Resistance Army that lasted from 1987-2007, disrupting their lives and livelihoods, and abducting thousands of children. We owe deep gratitude to the many who offered their friendship and shared their experiences with us not only involving the war, but even more importantly, their survival and work to rebuild their post-war society. We honour their resilience. The proceeds of this book will all go to the Ugandan women authors' organisations described in this book, and to girls' scholarships.

Contents

Acknowledgements ix
List of Abbreviations x
Foreword xi
Introduction xv

1. **Dynamics of hope from an international perspective** 1
   Editorial perspectives and challenges, and
   a framework of hope 3
   Who are we, and why are we involved in this work? 9
   Limitations of this work 22

2. **Lira District, then and now** 25
   Before the war 26
   During the war 28
   Post-war 32

3. **Concerned Parents Association** 35
   Eunice 36
   Consy 40

4. **Women of Lira** 46
   Recommendations: What can be done to improve
   the lives of women and girls in the community? 53

5. **Te-cwao Youth and Elderly Association** 62
   Success Stories 66
   The Piggery Project 67
   Development Plans 68
   Women's Cooperatives in Northern Uganda 69

6. A time for healing 73
7. Children in schools and expressive art therapy 80
    Capturing invisible time 83
    St Katherine Secondary School for Girls............................. 85
    Rachele Comprehensive School 91
    Barlonyo Technical and Vocational Institute 93
8. Lives in pictures.. 103
9. Women Achievers group and King Solomon
    Nursery and Primary School... 112
10. Community needs – teacher, radio talk
    show host, and psychologist... 117
    Origins of the gender programme....................................... 120
    Impacts of the gender programme...................................... 122
    New developments: Q FM and the
    community connection... 123
    PsychoAid International 124
11. Cold water: From regional to international documents,
    and the future women and girls of Lira.......................... 125

Suggested resources.. 135

References 140

Kickstarter contributors 145

Index.. 147

Acknowledgements

There are many people who made this book possible. Together, we thank the many people we have come to know and care for deeply in Lira, Uganda. They include our co-authors and many others whose trust and help have made our time in Lira rewarding and valuable. Many of the women we have come to cherish wrote chapters for this book, and we are humbled and grateful for those necessary contributions. To those who have not written, but who have become a part of our lives; and also to the men who contribute to furthering the cause of women's rights, we offer our gratitude and thanks.

We are grateful to our editors, Mariam Nakisekka and Bernard Atuhaire, for their excellent advice and encouragement. We are also grateful to our publisher, Tom Tibaijuka, and all the staff at Fountain Publishers for turning our manuscript into a polished book.

The editors and authors wish to thank everyone who contributed to the book's kickstarter campaign. Without them, this book might not have been published. Those who contributed $20 or more are listed individually at the end of this book.

Additionally, Jody McBrien wishes to give special thanks to her co-editor, Julia Byers, for her highly generous donation to begin production in March 2015.

List of Abbreviations

BTVI:	Barlonyo Technical and Vocational Institute
CBO:	Community Based Organisation
CEDAW:	Convention on the Elimination of all Forms of Discrimination Against Women
IGA:	Income Generating Activities
JRP:	Justice and Reconcilliation Project
LDA:	Lango Region Development Agenda
MDGs:	Millennium Development Goals
TYEA:	Te-cwao Youth and Elderly Association
UNFPA:	United Nations Fund for Population Activities
UPE:	Universal Primary Education
USE:	Universal Secondary Education
VSLA:	Village Savings and Loan Association
WAN:	Women's Advocacy Network

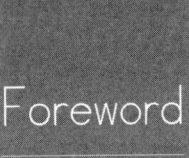

Foreword

In Leblango, there is a saying: *Gwok pe lelo icak iyi awottere,* "A dog never leaps with joy at the milk in the stomach of its friend." Loosely translated, it means that people can only be happy when they experience contentment at a personal level. In other words, gratification comes from self-actualisation. From the surface, the saying may seem to encourage selfishness and individualism- qualities that are frowned upon in Lango. However, when one analyses the overall implication of that individual satisfaction, it ceases to be selfish and individualistic and transcends to the community as well. This is because individual success is viewed in Lango as part of the community's success. There are plenty of other sayings that also encourage the spirit of communality, collectiveness, and togetherness in Leblango. The saying *Dako Nywal inyeke,* "A woman gives birth with the help of her co-wife"; or *Oyo alwak golo ot,* "Many rats ease the work of burrowing a house," testify to the need for working together. The more hands there are, the lighter the work. I relate these sayings to the success and satisfaction that comes with seeing the women of Lira writing their own stories in this book with the motivation and support from scholars and researchers from outside Lira.

If the women of Lira had chosen not to tell their stories, others would have told them on their behalf and, therefore, they would have been the ones to miss the fulfilment that comes with sucking their own milk and feeling the enormous satisfaction. However, Lira women chose to tell their stories alongside those of their guests. The multiple voices that come out in this book: voices from the outsiders telling their own personal stories as well as the stories of the insiders, voices of women and girls of Lira, telling their own stories, all these make this book a very rich collection of stories of women who succeed in representing their own life stories foremost, as well as the stories of other women who may not have had the opportunity to speak for themselves. In this way, *Cold Water: Women and Girls of Lira, Uganda* becomes a great resource representing a collection of Langi women's experiences of the LRA war and its aftermath. It is an archival resource that future generations and scholars can read in order to know what went on during and after the LRA war. *Cold Water: Women and Girls of Lira, Uganda* exceptionally brings Langi women to the forefront and situates them as actors who were part of the LRA war saga.

This collection of stories on women and girls of Lira should be mandatory reading for scholars in Women and Gender Studies, African Studies, Peace and Conflict Studies, Education, Art and Therapy as well as scholars of International Relations, to mention a few. Most of the textbooks, biographies, and documentaries that have been made about the LRA war have brought out the experiences of the Acholi more than the Langi. This is rightly so because the LRA war originally started from Acholi region. It is important to note, however, that the LRA war eventually spilled over and affected all the ethnic groups neighbouring Acholiland. How were these people affected? How do we get to learn about their stories? This book provides such an opportunity for readers to know how this war affected the women and girls from the Lango sub-region. Information included here is based on the editors' area of study, with recognition that other northern regions included in the Peace, Recovery and Development Plan (PRDP) have been devastated by both war and retracted donor investments for post-war aid.

Through Jody McBrien's and Julia Byer's collaboration with Betty Regina Okwir, Aceng Emma Okite, Consy Ogwal, Akwang Eunice, Kia Betty, Acen Eunice, and Acan Grace, Langi women's experiences and perceptions of the LRA war come to be narrated. The contributing authors not only recall the hopelessness felt during the war; they move steps further and narrate stories of hope and stories about how the women are rebuilding their lives after the war. These are stories of hope amidst past despair. Every page is crammed with emotionally wrapped recollections of personal experiences, which become political because they move beyond the individuals and show how communities get affected through what happens in the lives of individuals. These are the kind of stories that ought to be shared, because they show how communities can be rebuilt even where hope seemed to have been lost.

The writing style innovatively juxtaposes the experiences of two "outsider" scholars, Jody Lynn McBrien and Julia Gentleman Byers, with the narratives of "insider" Ugandan Langi women and girls who experienced the LRA war first hand between 1987 and 2007. Jody and Julia had come to Uganda to apply their knowledge of art as therapy for the broken girls and women of Lira, but they ended up doing more than offering psychosocial support through their art therapy classes to schoolgirls. They, in addition, created a social network that touched the lives of ex-child victims of the LRA war. Through their contact with the Langi women, more advances have been made. Consy Agwal has not only furthered the work of Women Achievers Group; she has also created a school in a rural area where children previously had no opportunity for education. Emma has expanded her radio talk shows that offer community assistance and began the first psychological services for the Lira community called PsychoAid International. Eunice Akwang has expanded the work and outreach of her community based organisation, Te-cwao. The weaving of the insider/outsider experience creatively facilitates a fusion where the stories begin to complement each other. This book is a product of that fusion. Like it is implied in the metaphorical title of the book, these women's words provide cool relief like that provided by the spring cold water, to the otherwise parched up dry stories of pain, struggle that are laced with stories of hope, stories of endurance and the fight to make life better for Langi women and girls after the LRA war.

Florence Ebila
Lecturer, Women and Gender Studies
Makerere University, Kampala, Uganda

Introduction

Jody McBrien and Julia Byers

> In the process of walking back, walking to Sudan, coming back to Uganda, we had to crisscross the country of Uganda and Sudan like that with the rebels. Sometimes when we shed our water, when a friend urinated, we would struggle and fight for that urine. Because you have to drink that urine for your own survival. If you don't drink, you can die. ~ Eunice Acen, interview

There is a place at Karuma Falls where Kony's soldiers captured the bridge, shutting off national forces from the south that fought to protect the people in the northern villages. It is heavily guarded, and no photographs are allowed of the bridge. However, the power of the Nile is stunning there, and we slowed down as we crossed in a dusty car, trying to furtively snap a few memories. On the other side, a female soldier holding a machine gun waved us off the road and glared into the car windows.

"I'm thirsty," she said, after a moment. Fearing that she might confiscate our cameras or prevent our travel, Julia offered the water bottle stored in her knapsack for the long drive ahead. Our two male African drivers gazed nervously into the rear view mirror at us. "It's hot, and I have to be here all day," the soldier said, wiping her brow. The wild current of the water behind and below us resonated with our own wild thoughts about our near future. She sipped the cold water slowly, her eyes fixed on us. Finally, she stepped back and waved us on.

In Uganda, where water supplies are scarce or contaminated, women and girls are the ones who must look for alternative sources of water for domestic use. In many countries of the world, they walk for miles, returning to their homes with containers of the life-saving liquid on their heads to use for cooking, washing dishes, clothes, and bodies; and boiling the rest to use for drinking. In these countries, during both war and peace, pure, cold water is a precious commodity.

The website water.org notes that "In just one day, 200 million work hours are consumed by women collecting water for their families. This is equivalent to building 20 Empire State Buildings *every day*" (http://water.org/water-crisis/water-facts/women/). Women are bearers of life, not only through childbirth, but through their connection to water and carrying it long distances for cooking, bathing and cleaning. When they unite, they can also be a powerful and a formidable force for change.

Like the cold, refreshing water we require but barely notice in the United States, the women of Lira, Uganda, have gone unnoticed. And yet, they are as essential to their society as the water they carry. In our work with children and families affected by war, we have discovered that women are the cornerstones in their societies. Frequently widowed or deserted by men who have handled their post-war trauma with anger, helplessness, or depression, the women raise their children as well as the orphans of their relatives or former neighbours. They are able to eke out a living by selling what they make with their hands or grow on their small plots of land. Some are sold as child brides by their families for as little as a bag of beans; and many have been raped by rebel soldiers. Their bodies frequently tell stories of war's trauma by the cut and burn scars on their arms and faces. In spite of these struggles, the women form groups and cooperatives that encourage and support one another through their days of farming, sewing, weaving, crafting jewellery, and plaiting hair together. Others have become managers of Community-Based

Organisations (CBOs) or teachers and leaders at schools. They use the small income they make to pay for school fees and maintain a home for themselves and their children, encouraging the girls to stay in school, and working towards equal rights for women. Their organisations encourage and support improved health conditions, educational opportunities, agriculture, media, and politics (Tripp and Kwesiga 2002).

Northern Uganda suffered under a brutal civil war led by Joseph Kony and his Lord's Resistance Army (LRA) between 1987-2007, resulting in the deaths of more than 100,000 people and displacement of nearly two million (Ellison 2006). Tens of thousands of children, called "night commuters," walked miles every evening and morning to sleep in urban night shelters that were somewhat less attacked by the LRA. Estimates of child abductions range from 24,000 to 75,000 (ICTJ 2014; Pham, Vinck and Stover 2007; UN n.d.; US Department of State 2012). These abductions include children as young as six years old, taken from their homes, village centres, or schools, and forced to become soldiers, servants, and sex slaves. The abuse they experienced was severe. Sometimes they were forced to kill their own families so that they would have no one to return to if they tried to escape. They were tortured or murdered for refusing to obey orders. They were starved and dehydrated, often forcing them to drink their own urine or eat raw flesh. Girls were raped, repeatedly.

Our book is about women's voices in an often forgotten part of the world, where struggles are deeply embedded within the fabric of everyday dress. We arrived with expectations of sharing some international aid in the form of expressive art for girls in secondary schools, which became a broader context that many readers of our book will find compelling. We returned with students' drawings of brutal killings, of coffins, and of flowers symbolising hope; and with the narratives of women who tirelessly insist on more than mere survival. The Lira women's initiatives and courage are the underpinnings of women around the world seeking equality, dignity, and basic human rights. This book is, in part, addressed to educators, psychologists, administrators, and human services professionals. But more simply, it is written for the hopes of all women in solidarity as we support one another to attain the respect and dignity that are a basic human right.

Images of cold water were ever present throughout all of our trips to Lira, from our needs to hydrate and to cool down, to our awareness of girls fetching water at pumping stations and carrying it on their heads to homes that could be miles from the source. We experienced awe when our journey took us over torrential Nile River rapids and fear when our own journey was threatened by the female soldier who demanded cold, fresh water from us. Other water associations came to us over our days in Lira: the metaphor of water as fertility (Ugandan females have the third highest fertility rate in the world), the tears in women's eyes as they recalled murdered children and relatives, the sweat on our bodies as we worked through hours of hot weather with no air-conditioned reprieve. The female students we worked with needed water to paint with the water colours we had brought for them to use for the first time. That water, mixed with the colourful paints, told the stories of hope amidst acute suffering in the students' artworks.

The aphorism "still water runs deep" is also applicable, as the narratives of the women of Lira and the Lango sub-region come from the depths of their souls. Like the true depths of still water, their stories are typically hidden from strangers. People who survive wars are often understandably wary of foreigners dropping in to uncover their stories. Jody has travelled to Lira four times since November 2010, during which she has maintained contact with people she first interviewed. Although this was only Julia's second trip to Uganda, she is no stranger to impoverished and war-torn zones, having travelled 23 times to Israel and Palestine to teach and work with those affected by the on-going conflict. We both believe in a concept of reciprocity, in which we offer something back to those individuals who entrust us with the details of their lives. For us, this has meant organising workshops for students and adults in Lira. We presented, together with two of the chapter writers; Aceng Emma Okite and Kia Betty, at the International Consortium for Social Development Conference held in Kampala in July 2013. Finally, we are writing this book to make public the trauma, courage, and triumphs of the remarkable women of Lira. All proceeds from the sales of this book will go to the women authors' organisations and to girls' scholarships.

Although our book focuses its pages on the struggles and contributions of women, we recognise many valiant efforts of Ugandan men who support women's efforts and rights. Among them are Olong Raymond, the director of Alternative to Violence Centred Organisation for Humanity (AVCOH) in Lira, and his excellent staff: Obunga Robert, Okello Godfey, and Akello Sandra, Martin Atim, among them. The stated objectives of AVCOH are the following:

- Increasing awareness and support for women's rights;
- Increasing awareness and support for women's psychosocial development;
- Improving the life skills and livelihood skills of women; and
- Increasing protection of women.

The work of AVCOH includes extensive HIV/AIDS trainings, counselling, and testing. The staff is also working to improve the quality of water in their region.

Another important male leader is Gira Emmanuel, the Director of Teens Media. He works with young people in Lira to present workshops at secondary schools about social issues facing youth, including HIV/AIDS and domestic violence. He also hosts a radio show on Radio Wa that provides audio plays for youth about social issues. The radio station also offers a women's programme.

Christopher Jojogle is the Director of Freidis Rehabilitation and Disabled Centre in Lira. He and his staff work tirelessly to aid the rehabilitation of youth returning from the bush and to provide therapy and advocacy for children with medical impairments that are often overlooked in the society. A new acquaintance in 2013, Charles Morgan Kisitu is the President of 1000 Shades of Green Tour and Safari Company in Kampala. His company (www.gogreensafari.com) works to provide environmentally responsible tours. With his profits, Morgan has built an orphanage and elementary school. He is the proud single father of two boys and told us with excitement that he was adopting a girl who he found in a terrible slum in Nairobi. And there is Okwir Betty's husband, Deputy Mayor of Lira Municipal Council, Okwir Johnson Dengai. There was not a dry eye in the house when he talked at length of his love and devotion to his wife, one of this book's authors.

This is but a small sample of the men in Uganda who support women and make a positive difference towards equality for all in their country. We have chosen, however, to record the stories of women in this book, as they are the ones who have historically gone unheard.

Chapter One creates the framework by which the editors, Drs Jody McBrien and Julia Byers, reflect on their outsider perspectives and theories of cross-cultural research. We articulate theories that can help readers understand the profound issues in a society desperate to create full and meaningful lives against the canvas of a brutal and senseless civil war, and we explore the concept of hope. In exchange for our women colleagues' honesty in telling their stories, we offer personal insights to our lives by way of explaining our backgrounds that draw us to this work. We also reflect on our own sense of place and the concept of White power and privilege as we work to support and empower the women of Lira.

In Chapter Two, Aceng Emma Okite and Kia Betty offer a brief history of Lira District and the Lango sub-region. Emma is a history teacher and counsellor at St Katherine Secondary School for Girls in Lira, a residential school for 1,000 secondary school girls; a volunteer hostess for two community talk radio programmes; and the founder and executive director of a new Lira NGO, PsychoAid International. Its goal is to offer counselling services to underserved residents in the Lango sub-region, eventually expanding to other regions in northern Uganda. Betty is a member of Women Achievers and a sub-county chief settling cases of domestic violence, child abuse, rape, drunkenness, defilement, separation and divorce, and land disputes. In this chapter, the women recount the impact of civil war between the Uganda People's Defence Forces (UPDF) and Kony's Lord's Resistance Army by describing particular hardships faced by women in Lira District. They also examine needs going forward as the community engages in post-war reconstruction.

Chapter Three gives voice to the Concerned Parents Association. Acen Eunice had two sisters abducted from St Mary's School in Aboke, and she worked with the Concerned Parents Association to help returned children reintegrate into society. Agwal Consy recounts her tireless determination not to give up hope for the safe return of her daughter, Grace, one of the thirty Aboke girls[1] who were abducted by the LRA. Eunice and Consy tell their stories of fear and courageous, relentless action to gain governmental and international attention to release abducted children. As parents, both women share their courage, grief, and work to reintegrate returned children into their homes and communities, as well as their sorrow for those who never returned.

---

[1] The Aboke girls were students attending St Mary's School in Aboke when the LRA raided in 1996. They initially took 139 girls at night. Sister Rachele bravely followed in pursuit, through trails in mine fields. Upon reaching the rebels, she begged for their release. The commanders returned 109 of the girls to her but kept 30. Five girls died in captivity, and one is still missing. Many bore commanders' children. Some were eventually released; others managed to escape (such as Grace Acan, author of Chapter Six).

In Chapter Four, Kia Betty and Aceng Emma Okite examine the role of women in Lango culture with particular attention given to post-war social structure. The women recount multiple events that have resulted in the dissemination of academic and health-related education to women in remote areas. They also offer a section on current women who have risen above the oppression of patriarchy to serve in leadership positions of commerce, education, medicine, and politics. These women are role models to girls and young women.

In Chapter Five, Eunice Akwang's story and her grass roots organisation Te-cwao represent women's empowerment through the creation of economic cooperatives. Founded in 2006, Te-cwao is similar to many community-based organizations (CBOs), which bring together women who are widows and young mothers (Te-cwao includes men as well) to train them for diverse vocations such as bead-making, weaving, tailoring, livestock keeping, crop farming, and beekeeping. Co-op training in such trades creates an income for the members, enabling them to support their families and keep their children in school. Their strings of beads are both literal and metaphorical objects to the community that connect and create hope to make a difference in members' lives.

Acan Grace, one of the Aboke girls, relates the details of her escape from the rebels with her infant daughter in Chapter Six. She concentrates on how she has moved beyond her traumatic life experience to be a graduate in Developmental Studies at Gulu University and a leader of the Women's Advocacy Network (WAN), consisting of nine women's groups that are a part of the Justice and Reconciliation Project in Gulu.

Through numerous interviews at schools, rehabilitation centres, and community organisations, McBrien describes the background of the history and dilemmas of school-aged girls in schools in Chapter Seven, including drop-outs and initiatives to keep girls in schools. Thousands of girls are unable to receive secondary education because parents cannot afford the school fees, so young women often marry early or work to support their single parent households with younger siblings. Byers describes our international efforts to empower young women to make meaning of their lives, relationships, and hopes beyond experienced trauma. Through therapeutic-based arts initiatives, this chapter documents our awareness of the power of cross-cultural time and how trauma frequently freezes memories. Working with local artefacts and animal symbols, the arts intervention builds a concretising creativity as a form of agency and resilience in the girls' development. "*Etic*" (outsider perspective) and "*emic*" (insider, or native perspective) approaches to multicultural awareness reflect the challenges of international intervention.

Chapter Eight includes a selection of girls' artwork from the schools at which we conducted workshops: Barlonyo Technical and Vocational Institute, St Katherine Secondary School for Girls, Rachcle Secondary School, and Barlonyo Technical and Vocational Institute. Some are accompanied by the girls' writings or narrations. The images reflect the depth of the pain they still carry post-war, as well as the hope they carry for their futures.

Chapters Nine and Ten focus on initiatives to confront current social dilemmas. Founded in 2012, the Women Achievers Organisation seeks to provide encouragement to girls and education to families to keep their girl children in school. Director, Regina Betty Okwir, and others are working to reduce the drop-out rate and reframe the importance of providing education for girls. Betty also founded the King Solomon Nursery and Primary School, also described in Chapter Nine. Aceng Emma Okite describes the women's and community initiatives at Radio Rhino and Quality FM as they play a major role in educating women about their health and welfare. These volunteer efforts have resulted in the dissemination of contemporary mental health counselling to help comfort women who are isolated and afraid. Emma is the host of these shows, which she does on a volunteer basis. With few mental health counsellors available in schools or clinics, and a dearth of medically trained mental health doctors in Lira, there are few resources for women and girls. This is also why Emma opened PsychoAid International, providing counselling, mentorship, psychosocial support, and vocational training for girls, to help them overcome various stresses in their lives.

Our concluding commentary in Chapter Eleven bridges the lessons learned from the narrative inquiries with recommendations from local to international policies. If post-war issues are addressed, economic development can improve, thus raising the aspirations and possibilities of the girl-child. This volume of voices adds to the emerging efforts of women to go beyond merely surviving, to thriving. The implications of the research – and of the women whose lives are depicted here – go far beyond Uganda, offering hope to women in other war-torn nations.

Finally, we recommend a number of resources for learning more about the LRA war, Ugandan society, and women in Uganda.

Although post-traumatic stress disorder is a well-known syndrome, its opposite, "post-traumatic growth," (PTG) is less commonly discussed. Richard Tedeschi and Lawrence Calhoun both coined the term PTG and have pioneered this research since 1996 (1996, 2010; see also Calhoun, Cann, and Tedeschi 2010). They define it as "the experience of positive change resulting from the struggle with major life crises" (2010). Further, the researchers believe it is based on "the disruption of one's assumptive beliefs, rather than the characteristics of the [traumatic] event itself" (Calhoun, Cann, and Tedeschi 2010, ch. 1). Although the concept is ancient, research scales to investigate it were not introduced until the mid-1990s. In recent years, the researchers have investigated both universal and particular characteristics of PTG in international contexts. One finding is the importance of culture and cultural values in encouraging this kind of transcendence from trauma. With resilient women of Lira, we have found these contexts in their beliefs in their community, their religious faith, and the solidarity of women, as they will detail in the chapters to follow.

The depth of our combined experiences cemented our resolve to give back to the Lira community through co-editing and producing the voices of strong women of Lira who took the initiative to be part of the solution for positive change. We hope that our efforts serve to empower less privileged women to be heard in a global context.

The beat of Ugandan music played as we collected stories for this book before returning to our homes in Boston and Sarasota, and the gentle breeze let us breathe deeply as we left the land and people we have come to love. The proceeds of this book will be given to support the work of women and education for girls and women in Lira. We hope to provide university scholarships and international teacher/counsellor exchanges with the Western continents. We thank you for celebrating the advancement of women who desire a better future for themselves and their children.

Dynamics of hope from an international perspective

Jody McBrien, Julia Byers, and Amy Huffaker

TO BE HOPEFUL in bad times is not just foolishly romantic. It is based on the fact that human history is a history not only of cruelty, but also of compassion, sacrifice, courage and kindness.

What we choose to emphasise in this complex history will determine our lives. If we see only the worst, it destroys our capacity to do something. If we remember those times and places—and there are so many—where people have behaved magnificently, this gives us the energy to act, and at least the possibility of sending this spinning top of a world in a different direction.

And if we do act, in however small a way, we don't have to wait for some grand utopian future. The future is an infinite succession of presents, and to live now as we think human beings should live, in defiance of all that is bad around us, is itself a marvelous victory."
~ Howard Zinn (2006, p. 270)

Many books focus on the tragedies resulting from Joseph Kony and his Lord's Resistance Army's (LRA) brutal twenty-year war in northern Uganda: *First Kill Your Family, The Night Wanderers, Stolen Angels, Child to Soldier, Aboke Girls, Girl Soldier,* and others. But there is little focusing on post-war reconstruction and attempts to maintain peace in the region since Kony's departure in 2007. This book focuses on a small group of women in Lira, Uganda, who have made multiple personal sacrifices in their attempts to rebuild their community and support girls after surviving more than two decades of war; and on girls in three secondary schools in Lira/Lango sub-region who are trying to rebuild their lives. We recognise that there are many local community organisations throughout northern Uganda that are involved in these efforts. We have focused on the women and girls we have come to know through repeated visits to Lira since 2010 in order to provide their detailed descriptions, recognising that our acquaintances represent the efforts of many Ugandan women throughout the war-affected regions.

It may seem incomprehensible to Western readers to imagine finding hope in a region in which nearly two million people lived in two hundred and forty-seven internally displaced persons' (IDP) camps throughout the north (UNHCR 2012) – some for two decades, and some who were born in the camps and have known nothing but war and fear throughout their childhoods. It is a region in which LRA rebels raided schools, villages and camps – abducting tens of thousands of children and youth. They brutally killed adults and abducted the children to become rebel soldiers or sex slaves to the commanders. Life in the IDP camps was characterised by hunger and disease due to lack of water, sanitary facilities and healthcare. There were high rates of domestic violence and rape. Local schools were consolidated into giant, inadequate educational spaces in camps with insufficient numbers of teachers and complete lack of discipline. Upon returning to villages post-war, residents found themselves at the mercy of land grabs and were often unable to prove their ownership through deeds or other official paperwork. There are four land tenure systems in Uganda – Mailo, leasehold, freehold, and customary. Those who purchase land easily confuse the varying conditions. Especially post-war, people have taken advantage of these differing conditions, and young people whose parents were killed have an especially hard time regaining their family land.

Thousands of children became orphans through war deaths or AIDS or other diseases; and women were widowed by similar causes. Years of warfare decimated infrastructure of community and private structures. In frustration and despair, many men turned to violence and alcohol.

The Zinn quote that opens this chapter speaks directly to women and men leaders we have met in Lira, people who work in voluntary organisations, teachers who go without pay for two to three months at a time, those who struggle without money or other resources to educate community members about HIV/AIDS, to combat domestic violence, and to encourage parents to send their girls to school. Some of our acquaintances were themselves captured by rebels. Others suffered through their own children's captivity; all were affected by the years of war and its traumatising effects on their lives.

It would be easy to sink into despair after losing family, land and the few possessions they owned prior to the war in this already high-poverty region, and many have. However, we met many who have risen above despair to act for a better future for northern Uganda. We chose to focus on the women, traditionally and historically viewed as second-class citizens in this society. The women we have come to know work as teachers, counsellors, and directors of local organisations to create self-sustaining ways to better the lives of girls and women in terms of education, healthcare, employment and psychological wellbeing.

Editorial perspectives and challenges, and a framework of hope

What is our place, White university professors from the United States, in understanding and publishing the stories of the Ugandan women who inspire us? This question is central to us as editors in our desire that this book be about the women and girls of Lira, and not about us. Thus, we open with a chapter that includes some theory, self-disclosure and limitations of this book in an attempt to address the challenges of cross-cultural and cross-racial work. We do this not to turn the spotlight on ourselves as editors, but to make the distinction of our goal to be "research instruments," as opposed to using our "research as self-expression" (Lawrence-Lightfoot and Davis 1997, p. 86).

Chandra Mohanty's (1988) seminal work on Western women's critiques of "third world" women informs how we view ourselves as researchers and editors of this work. She rightfully criticised the work of Western feminist scholars who viewed their peers in developing countries as "ignorant, poor, uneducated, tradition-bound, family oriented, victimised, etc." (p. 56). Many of the women and girls who have written chapters for this book, or whom we discuss, are poor; and many have been victims of the rebels or of their own husbands. But they are far from the stereotype of victimised objects with no agency. Indeed, the women populating this book have been subjected to numerous forms of abuse: women kidnapped by the LRA; women whose children were kidnapped; women who were burned or otherwise scarred by the LRA; one woman who fought off a man hired to kill her; women whose husbands have chosen to leave or take up with other women, often taking their children with them; and more. What makes their narratives important is that they have resisted the injustices of the war and of decades of gender inequity. They assert their agency and act on their beliefs for a better future for themselves and the children of Uganda. Writers of the chapters have carved out important leadership roles – creating reciprocal agencies between widows and orphans and schools; building schools in places where children formerly had no place to go for education; designing psychosocial services in communities that previously had no such service; helping women formerly abducted by the LRA rebuild their lives; and more. Through their actions, they provide mentorship and support for the girls in their communities and beyond.

In Mohanty's (2002) response to her 1986 article, "Under Western Eyes," she prefers terms "one-third world" and "two-thirds world" over "North/South" or "Western/developing" because the older terms presume geographical distances between the "haves" and "have nots" when, in fact, communities of marginalised women are found in wealthy capitalist countries as well as in poor ones. She cites Shiva's (2000, 1997) work on ways in which globalisation and corporatisation further impoverishes and marginalises women and girls:

> The effects of these governing bodies [such as the WTO, World Bank, and IMF, and so on] on poor people around the world have been devastating. In fundamental ways, it is girls and women round the world, especially in the Third World/South, that bear the brunt of globalisation. Poor women and girls are hardest hit by the degradation of environmental conditions, wars, famines, privatisation of services and deregulation of governments, the dismantling of welfare states, the restructuring of paid and unpaid work, increasing surveillance and incarceration in prisons, and so on. And that is why a feminism without and beyond borders is necessary to address the injustices of global capitalism. (Mohanty 2002, p. 514)

We observed this in Lira, as development there has not improved the living conditions of local residents. For instance, the largest factory in town is a grain milling plant, owned by an Indian corporation. The owners keep the prices for corn at a level that keeps local farms in perpetual poverty. There is a remarkable mall being constructed on a main road to replace the former shacks that contained Lira's main marketplace. However, the company contracted to build the structure is "Arab Contractors." Although we were told that the local people are expected to use the new space for their shops, one wonders if they will be able to afford the rent. In this book, we have concentrated on the microcosm of women and girls in Lira and the surrounding villages. However, it is important to remain aware of the larger international impact on the lives of the local people. Mohanty goes on to state that "activists and scholars must also identify and re-envision forms of collective resistance that women, especially in their everyday communities, enact in their everyday lives" (p. 515).

In an article I co-authored with a young Bosnian refugee woman who was a participant in one of my studies when she was just in junior high school (Besic and McBrien 2012), we used Lawrence-Lightfoot and Davis's (1997) theories of "portraiture" as a way to understand research about human lives and how we could understand one another. As this work is also pertinent to this current book about struggle and redemption, and Lawrence-Lightfoot and Davis's work offers "a path through the dilemma of personal relationships to participants with the method of portraiture". I will reproduce a section of the journal article here:

> Lawrence-Lightfoot and Davis began their book with an explanation of the main tenets of the method, which include a search for what is "good and healthy" (p. 9) as opposed to the traditional deficit model; a voice for the subjects of the study; an attempt to not only inform, but also inspire; the necessity of context; the inevitability of intervention. "In the process of creating portraits, we enter people's lives, build relationships, engage in discourse, make an imprint. . ." (p. 11). As a result, the researcher is also faced with "ethical dilemmas and a great moral responsibility" (p. 11). How can the researcher portray the lives of the subjects without getting in the way? How accurate is the work? Would similar results occur if the researcher had not been present in the lives of her subjects? Answers to such questions can only be conjecture. (Besic and McBrien 2012, p. 3)

A key to portraiture work is to continually note the presence and the subjectivity of the researcher. As such, we view ourselves as subjects in the study along with the inspiring women who have taught us what it means to be an LRA war survivor and a leader in the post-war challenges to rebuild their society.

More from the article (Besic and McBrien 2012):

> Davis used a tale by Nicolaides, an artist and teacher, who imagined a man from Mars observing a landscape on Earth for the first time. Nicolaides reflected on how a drawing by the Martian would be different than a drawing of the same scene by a human because the Martian would be relating the objects in the scene to what he knew on Mars. Nicolaides concluded that the two artists' results would only be comprehensible, one to the other, at interconnections of similar experience. Davis related the story to portraiture. The image of the man from Mars (the outsider) portraying objects with which he has little or no familiarity is analogous to the situation in which the portraitist is forging relationships with individuals (insiders) whose experiences and environment may be entirely different from her own. How will the portrayal be intelligible if the experiential base of the portraitist does not include prior knowledge of the realities of the subject or actors on a site? (p. 176)

The answer, it seems, is two-fold: the researchers need to work over an extended time period to have more than a "tourist" perspective; and the researchers must extend power and privilege to those who know the landscape far better than they. This commitment creates the element of "empathetic regard," what Lawrence-Lightfoot and Davis say occurs when one asks the question: "If I were looking through the world through her eyes, what would I see?" (p. 146). It also resonates with Mohanty's (1988) opposition to a deficit model and belief in prioritising the words of participants from a culture rather than those of the researcher. These are the goals we hope to achieve in creating a portrait of women's and girls' lives in Lira.

The barbaric circumstances of Kony's abductions, killings, and disruption of social life challenged the core of what it means to be human. The resiliency of the women of Lira is, in part, found in the fact that they could choose to detach themselves from their surroundings in the expectancy that something had to change. Their ultimate freedom lives in the fact they can choose their attitude and response to the most unthinkable situations they experienced. Given a common Western perspective of the desire for retaliation and revenge, the Lira women's and girls' choices to forgive those who tortured and killed their families and themselves is nothing short of remarkable, and it deserves examination in a world gone mad with demonising the "Other."

Many researchers have written about psychological resilience, and there are common threads within the narratives shared in our book. For many children, a sense of resiliency and hope springs from childhood relationships that supported and encouraged the wellness of their growth and development. For others, the spontaneity of hope can spring from a vivid imagination developed as part of childhood development. For younger and older adults, psychologically bonding with people on both a concrete and spiritual or existential level is one of the most important elements of the marriage between hope and resilience in defining a sense of wholeness. So many orphans and injured people were impaired both physically and psychologically. The challenge of choosing to change attitudes and beliefs from wishing to actualising real possibilities remains the aspirational goal of the women in our book who chose to "move forward." They were all willing to take risks to be resourceful and accept their own personal responsibility to be attentive and open to new ideas. Often looking to the resilience of nature and their spiritual beliefs, each day represented a conscience choice to "move forward."

Over our collective trips to Lira, we found compelling stories that built our framework for hope and resiliency. First, the women identified with the horrific facts of their experiences and were witnessed by outsiders (Jody and Julia). Second, they chose to let go of the intrusive thoughts and debilitating numbness of vulnerability in restoring their lives. They used the arts and narrative interviews as a safe place to contain ambivalent emotions. Third, they chose to move forward with a "compassionate choice" (Woodall 2007), the choice to forgive those who caused them terrible harm and not allow the death and destruction of the past to hinder their hope for the future.

In the first stage, when trust had been developed with us, the "outsiders," their need to share the complexities of the traumatic experiences appeared paramount to gain a sense of validation and understanding. Through narratives, poetry, song, and collective sharing of universal suffering, their voices were heard. Our goal was to honour every person's sense of self as it was, not to enforce or traumatise, but to recognise the dignity of the experience.

In the second phase, letting go of residual emotions and choosing to experience "normalising" experiences of art and play were offered to provide opportunities for new perspectives, ideas and healthy, supportive community building opportunities. The arts-based activities served as an invitation to possibilities that had remained unspoken for both women and girl students. Bringing people together to negotiate and collaborate on new initiatives provided a healing approach in a despairing community. The imagination of the possible makes the collaboration of this book a reality.

The "moving forward" that Emma repeatedly chanted gave us all hope in our concerted efforts to celebrate the dignity of all. Apathy is the complete absence of wishing or hoping. Together, joining the African and international heritages, we felt empowered to join in the collective momentum of celebrating the women of Lira's need for positive change. Their spirit infused both Jody and me to make more authentic changes in our own professional and personal lives. Different and yet the same, we all chose to "move forward" to contribute in honouring the legacy of women's challenges. We looked into each other's eyes and knew the collective power of our womanhood.

Who are we, and why are we involved in this work?

Because we come from different academic backgrounds and experiences, we chose to separate this section into the unique situations and perspectives we confront as we consider our roles in Lira and the writing of this book.

Lawrence-Lightfoot and Davis (1997) encourage scholars to include their personal backgrounds by way of addressing their own perspectives and biases as researchers. Women of Lira have given us hours of their time to share their individual stories. By way of honouring their honesty, we disclose parts of our own backgrounds that shape our reasons for engaging in this work.

Jody

I am the product of a spunky mother and equally strong grandmothers, and of men who tended to be quiet, though wilful. My mother's side of the family is peopled with impoverished coal miners and tenant farmers. Mom was born in a one-room shack in Harlan, Kentucky, at a coal-mining camp. Her father, himself abused and a teenage runaway, was brutal in his reprimands when she and her friends would defiantly slide down the coal chute or lose their shoes in the nearby creek. He was also racist, nothing surprising for his background and socio-historical context. I have fond memories of him taking me to a lake to swim that he called "Jody's pond," and gulping down huge bowls of chocolate ice cream as he watched the weekend TV wrestling shows. His wife, my maternal grandmother, always had pork roast boiling on the stove, along with the best Southern cornbread one could find baking in the oven. She worked as a school janitor, and although I believe she was a tough and angry woman while Mom was a child, I knew her as a kind and loving person. Thus, my own roots begin in a place of poverty, one in which men were paid in coal company "scrip" rather than cash as a way of enslaving them to ruthless and unhealthy work.

My father's stock came as Irish peasant immigrants through Ellis Island and settled in Canada and the northern United States. His mother was the only white person to be born on Navy Island, a small island in the Niagara River where the family built a farm. I cherished visits to my see my great grandmother, who sang and taught me her favourite ballads from Ireland. I remember Dad's father as a quiet, very loving man who took me to Fort Erie Racetrack every summer to satisfy my love of horses and his passion for betting on the races. His wife, my Grandma Hazel, was as strong-willed a woman as I have ever known. I remember being with her as she was looking for a parking space at a department store. Another car pulled in from the other direction and took the spot she was eyeing. I will never forget her jumping out of the driver's seat to give that driver a piece of her mind! Perhaps, I see her determined character in the women I know in Lira, who are not interested in wasting time complaining, but rather charge through the obstacles in their way.

My own father emerged much like his quiet father, and Mom bore the traits of anger that could explode into outbursts at my brother and me when we were young. We were sent to live with my father's family the year that I began kindergarten, as my young parents struggled with reducing the anger in the house. This pattern of disquiet haunted me as I became a mother myself and strove to curb the abuse that could result from it. Perhaps, I relate to the remarkable forgiveness shown by the women in Lira who have let go of their deep anger and tragedy imposed by rebels and men who have treated them with unfairness and cruelty, as I, too, learned to stop blaming my parents for my depression in my 20s and 30s by understanding what drove it. Ultimately, we reconciled.

Sadly, attempts to keep a relationship did not work with my brother. His deep anger and resentment led him to alcoholism, and he feeds his pain by lashing out at his family. He is also a racist, causing a rift between his daughter and him, as she married an African American man and has four beautiful bi-racial children. Since the death of our father, I have chosen to sever my relationship to my brother, as I could no longer bear his cruelty to my mother and his taunts aimed at me for my work in Africa. In some ways, he bears resemblance to men in northern Uganda who lost themselves to alcohol and despair in the war years.

I travelled to Lira annually between 2010 and 2013, and I kept up e-mail connections and occasional phone calls with my contacts in the town between visits. I was not completely shocked by the physical poverty of much of Lira, as I had visited a Liberian refugee camp in Ghana earlier in 2010 and have also travelled to impoverished towns in the Caribbean and Central America. Still, a well-educated middle-class American is wealthy beyond measure in northern Ugandan villages, and I would be morally corrupt not to be affected by crumbling buildings and the lack of resources available to most of the area. More surprising for me was discovering the wealth of people's dreams to rebuild the town and region, and their hard work and dedication to make those dreams become reality.

In some ways, I see that attempts at Westernisation have further sullied the Lira community with toilets that do not flush, sinks that are frequently dry (and when flowing, do not produce potable water), and electric sockets that do not work. Disposable products unaccompanied by Western methods of recycling or well-engineered landfills have scarred the beautiful landscapes, now filled with open piles of plastic bottles, cellophane wrap, plastic bags, old tyres, and broken cell phones amidst decomposing rubbish. At the same time, I have noticed remarkable growth in Lira between my initial visit in 2010 and my recent trip in July 2013. Each time I visit Barlonyo, the improvements are visible: the school has a new building, expanded tilapia ponds, new chicken coops, a separate latrine for girls, and a preschool. Community efforts resulted in expansion of the Barlonyo Massacre Memorial by creating the concrete structure encompassing the mass graves of the people slaughtered there in 2004. In 2013, a museum to commemorate the massacre was in initial stages of construction. Back in Lira, a giant mall is being constructed to house the 100+ small businesses that were maintained in shack-like buildings in previous years (though, as mentioned earlier, this is a problematic issue of globalisation). Betty Okwir, a co-author of this book, has built a primary school for children who previously had no place to go for education. Eunice has extended the outreach of Te-cwao Youth and Elderly Association. Emma has added a second radio show and started a new organisation, PsychoAid International, to counsel community members in need.

What is my role in a place so different from my own home, and how can I both join with women I have come to know and love in Lira, and do no harm? Over breakfast at the Speke Resort Munyonyo, Kampala's most luxurious conference hotel and, somewhat ironically, the location of a social development conference I attended with Julia and several of the book's co-authors, this question became central as Julia and I considered ethical research and behaviours to bridge our vastly different cultures. I noticed ways in which my American English is judgmental as my husband Dick used the term "primitive cultures"; and I heard others at the conference using similar terms.

Dick, an avid *Star Trek* fan, used the phrase "the prime directive" when he discussed venturing into other cultures. He explained the fictional characters' goal was to not change the cultures they visited. This is akin to the anthropological debate begun in 1947 by the American Anthropological Association in its "Statement on Human Rights," which posed the following question: Given vast cultural differences, is it better to simply observe human life in diverse cultures, even when events observed would be considered brutal and inhumane in our own society; or to advocate for changes? Both counterpoints and ironies become quickly obvious in this on-going debate. Is it ethical to stand by as a young girl experiences Female Genital Mutilation (FGM), a time-honoured tradition in parts of the world? At the same time, can Westerners, especially those from the United States, dare stand in judgment when we allow our tax dollars to support the largest military in the world with policies that have condoned torture and full-scale spying on US citizens and that benefit our already-privileged citizens at the expense of our global brothers and sisters?

These are my contexts as I consider my attempts to understand the culture and relationships of a post-war area where people suffer from hunger and preventable diseases, and whose women hold their dignity in marriage even as their husbands leave them for 20-year olds and take their property and/or their children. I find myself constantly questioning the motives behind my words and suggestions. Are the suggestions I make to a woman to help her improve her life going to truly help or hinder her situation? If she does not accept or cannot achieve the goal I speak of, have I simply left her with more suffering than had the suggestion never crossed her mind? These dilemmas are always in my mind as I work with the women I have come to care for deeply. Unfortunately, good intentions can cause great pain.

In the US, we cling to the myth that anyone can climb the sociocultural ladder if he or she works hard enough. As an educational sociologist, I know that myth can victimise many striving to enter the machine of middle class life without middle class cultural capital. And as a comparative educator, I know that one cannot simply import a system that may work in Tampa, Florida, and expect it to produce the same results in Lira, Uganda. There are too many cultural contexts supporting the successful system in Tampa that are not found in the town of Lira. My own Western thoughts are forever clouded by my US status and lifestyle, no matter how hard I struggle against it.

For this reason, both Julia and I chose to maintain the voice in the writings and the interviews of our Ugandan co-authors as closely as possible. When I submit journal manuscripts, evaluators of my articles often complain that I do not sufficiently critique the comments of those I interview. In response, I find myself wondering how I, a White middle-class woman, can better restate the words of a refugee or a Ugandan woman or child. How could my interpretations possibly be superior to their lived experiences? Over the years, I have become more disillusioned with traditional Western research expectations. I find it harder to think of myself as a researcher at all, as the role creates a problematic imbalance in power relations.

Regarding refugee and war survivor studies, I favour care, understanding, and meaning over scientific methods that create distance between the researcher and the participants. I fault on the unscientific side of creating relationships with the women whose words created this book. Had those relationships brought about wishes from the women that the stories not be published-I would have been simply been glad to have earned their confidence. I had this happen previously with a refugee who has become a friend of mine. I misinterpreted some of her words, and she pulled out of my study. It was ok; I was simply glad I could salvage the relationship, as it was far more important to me than the publication. Narratives such as the ones gathered here do not come from superficial trips to a country, conducting focus groups and interviews, and distributing surveys to those with whom I have no relationship. I was shocked when I listened to a US researcher at the conference in Kampala describe bringing students to Kenya to work and conduct studies when she had absolutely no contacts or entrance to the country or the village at which she planned to focus her work. She just assumed that they would be welcomed. I wondered, would this professor have made similar assumptions had she been conducting a study in Germany, for example, or even her own country, the United States? Such naïveté, though unintentional, disrespects people and communities in developing countries. The word "developing" is itself disturbing, as I ask the question: Developing towards what? Western standards? Why is Western culture considered "developed" over Southern and Eastern nations, given that "developed" also includes the connotation of "superior"?

I apply Nel Nodding's (2005) framework of care in the work I have done in Uganda. Just as she states that educational systems need to first concern themselves with producing caring, responsible young adults over youth who can ace standardised tests, so should work such as that in this book concern itself first with the welfare and care of the women populating these chapters. They are both this book, and they are more important than this book. If the pages do not allow Lira women's voices to be heard above the chatter of its Western editors, then we have failed. To this end, they are our co-authors and editors. Everything published here has the authors' full approval. As the contents are their stories, so the proceeds of the sales are theirs as well, and will be used to further the education and hope of the girls and women of Lira.

Julia

> A primary function of art and thought is to liberate the individual from the tyranny of culture. -Lionel Trilling (2009)

In *The Art and Science of Portraiture,* Lawrence-Lightfoot and Davis (1997) make the distinction between "self as research instrument" and "research as self-expression" (p.86). In our work to help tell the women of Lira's stories in this book, Jody and I recognise the importance of first examining our own life experiences and the ways in which they colour our stories so we may more capably present the voices of the women of Lira. Without examination, experiences that have shaped how we view ourselves and the world around us threaten to intrude on the stories we are witnesses to: our unexamined stories endanger ourselves as "instruments." The following section provides the reader with a glimpse into my personal story in order to understand the different lenses from which I work and to better understand the special place in my soul from which this book emerged.

The collective portraitures of Lira women who have lived the suffering and betrayal of unspoken horrors, yet today speak of resilience and hope, touch my being in ways that compel me to put their stories onto paper. Without romanticising our trips to Lira, I know Jody and I are forever changed by the profound "human clinical tales" of the brave women we have met (Sacks in Lawrence-Lightfoot and Davis 1997, p.5). I have personally experienced the power of the disenfranchised, the marginalised, and the oppressed through working with many refugees and immigrants in multiple countries. Having participated in 23 trips to Israel and Palestine to help those who grieve from the horrors of suicide bombers or the rubber-bullet wounds aimed at children to devastate theirs and their family's lives, life can be hardened. Similar, yet different from man-made violence, are people who have profound losses due to natural disasters. Working with those people who suffered loss either through the mudslide typhoons in the Philippines or the earthquakes in Turkey, everyone grieves.

I have often wondered why I repeatedly have been invited to help in foreign countries. My father, Walter Williams Charles Gentleman, was a corporal in the British Army who was sent to Palestine in WWII to serve as a communications officer. My mother, Margaret Joyce Lakeman Kelf, found herself and her parents seeking refuge in Iran during her adolescence. With the breakout of the First World War, her father, a British architect, was stationed in Tehran to help build the British Embassy. The project was delayed and extended and during my mother's developing young adult years, she was surrounded by a culture that deeply influenced her cultural sensitivities. A young foreign woman in a conservative country, the response to my mother's blossoming sexuality was a forced abortion and genital mutilation as punishment for cavorting with a high-powered Iranian man. My father's family was also affected by WWI. My grandfather's leg was blown off in the army conflicts. When he returned to England with his wooden leg, his new livelihood was as a truck driver. His wife, Aida, cleaned houses in between hiding in the backyard bomb shelter during the continuing war. One day, when she and her three children shivered in the cold brick shelter during a bomb scare, she ran back into the house, claiming that she had had enough. If they were meant to die, they would die together in their own home, not surrendering in a makeshift town dump.

Growing up in Canada, I was spared the conflicts of the old European dilemmas only to experience the rift between the French and English political conflicts. As the intensity of the separatist movement escalated, the societal demand was for Anglophones and immigrants to leave the country to make way for a more popular Québécoise vote.

During my first trip to Uganda, I was deeply affected by the colonial British school systems that still maintain a 1950's style and practice of education. Feeling ashamed of my British birth and lineage, I frequently felt triggered by the authoritarian nature of the archaic British educational rule, given my memory of examinations with little room for the discovery or love of learning. The children Jody and I saw, who were lucky enough to attend school, worked diligently mastering the basics of reading, writing and arithmetic, their diligence emblematic of hope for their future. With the extremely low pay and minimal education of many of the teachers, the best teaching appears to be delivered in a good faith effort. Even as I write these words, I am encumbered by my strong feelings that education can be so much more than just reading and math and recitation. Celebrating the local culture and wisdom has always been my bias, especially in places such as Uganda, where there is potential to enrich and motivate the lives of students who may be craving connection.

In examination of my own privileges, I also recognise how fortunate I was to be raised in a family that appreciates the arts. My father's claim to fame was his role as a special effects director in Stanley Kubrick's *2001 Space Odyssey*, and my mother was a ballroom dancing instructor. My own artistic development grew from helping my father paint animatronic cells for the Expo 67 World's Fair Pulp and Paper Expositions at the age of nine. Throughout my teenage and college years, I had the privilege of taking several art classes and creating work at the Canadian Conference of the Arts Association and with the faculty of Arts at McGill University. My initial undergraduate degree in Art Education provided me with the aesthetic sensibilities of using multiple art materials as forms of discovery, insight, and creativity. The thread of my personal and professional life has always been through the communication of the arts.

My entrance into sharing life with others is predicated upon developing a therapeutic alliance built on respect, trust and dignity. The creed of a mental health counsellor is to "do no harm." Similar to Jody's commentary of the "prime directive" of the Star Trek voyage to unknown places and cultures, as a foreigner, I aim to help and not hinder the environment in which I am welcomed into. My passport to Lira was Jody, who paved the way for me to be welcomed into the community as Jody's friend. My second trip was made without Jody, and was possible due to the friendships and connections established during our previous trip the year before. Through intimate conversations, such as my dinner with Emma in her home, I saw more clearly the issues that have created lasting residue from the massive disruption of individuals and families by Kony's army. I felt Emma's pride in her 21 year-old son who is now in college and finding a new direction in his life. I played with the HIV positive orphans who were abandoned by their abductee mothers and whom Emma took in as her own. I heard stories of family and kin who offered help from afar as Emma and others attempted to uphold their lives and protection of their children with dignity. I saw the love of family and friends in the photographs hung on the wall to remember "good days," as Emma put it. Her goal is to establish the first Ugandan International Psychological counselling aid services in Lira. This is a goal I know she will achieve because her vision is so compelling. As she drew a blueprint of what the new building structure would look like, I knew the lines on the page foreshadowed the actuality of achieving her dream.

> From my Ugandan journal entry July 11, 2012:
>
> As day turned into night, the red dust on the ground still hovered in every crack of the cement structures between Emma's home and

my transient hotel. It was as if the grit was waiting for the breeze. The heat finally broke, and a downpour of hot rain flooded the area overnight. The water saturated leaves, now painted by remnants of the clay dirt fragments, giving Lira another colour. As we drove down muddy, uneven roads, we witnessed how the yearned for, yet unanticipated rain left its mark on the landscape. Balancing between the harsh temperatures and stark areas, I couldn't help feel that the outside metaphors reflected the struggles that I felt inside.

So begins my journey into the land of metaphors and imagination in and through the arts and how we chose to incorporate them into our work with the women and girls of Lira. Drawing, painting, and building creative expressions have been profound healing tools for me, both personally and professionally. There are many critics who may ask what the role of a white middle-aged woman could be in facilitating arts-based workshops or art therapy informed sessions among the dark skins of African women and girls. In Uganda, reclaiming the role of the arts in culture to move beyond trauma demonstrates resilience in and of itself, and my role as facilitator was simply to witness that resilience. Perhaps, my role as a foreigner who cared enough to return to help the girls was enough to mute the stark differences between my own lived experience and that of the girls I had come back to see.

I was privileged to work with twelve girls at St Katherine Senior Secondary School for a second time and witness their growth and development over the previous year. During my second visit, I was more relaxed and felt more at ease with the girls and women who were so welcoming. I am not sure if it was my presence, or the new art materials and the opportunity to play via the arts that built a sense of normalcy in their lives (if only for a while). The girls seemed less preoccupied with school challenges or the dreaded feeling that family may or may not visit them on "Parents Day" that day as some families were too poor or lived too far away to visit their daughters. Or worse, some girls were orphaned or had little family left. So the art therapy session provided a metaphoric holding, a container where the community of women could giggle and share in the mystery of the arts. My hope is that the art materials provided each girl with a sense of autonomy and the acknowledgement of the tension between surviving in a very structured environment of the school, while living with the knowledge of the trauma in the past and daring to hope for the future. It was often difficult to understand the local accent of Leblango, and the girls were instructed to speak in English, appearing very self-conscious under the watchful eye of their teachers and the newcomer. Adding their own colours, words, and play of recycled art materials gave everyone a sense of portraying pictures without words. In a sense, the mental health creed of "do no harm" resonated with me as I deliberated in the tension between evoking narrative stories or sealing over traumatic thoughts, knowing the production and act of creating something perhaps offered an embodied sense of hope and change.

Amy

I had the privilege of working as Julia Byers' graduate assistant while earning my Masters at Lesley University while she and Jody were working on the *Cold Water* manuscript. I was honored to contribute to the book as a reader, researcher, and student editor, as I feel a deep sense of sorrow for refugees. I also feel amazement and gratitude for those who return to their communities to rebuild after the devastation of war, and the issues they face. I am humbled by the opportunity to work with strong, admirable women who have chosen to tell their stories in this book so that the rest of the world can find hope in their strength. I have a Master's degree in Theology from Drew Theological School and a Master's in Art Therapy from Lesley University. My background includes working in women's advocacy and human rights issues. I plan to continue addressing the needs of women through spirituality and art.

Limitations of this work

We recognise a number of issues that prevent our collaborative work from being all that we want it to be. At the same time, we also suggest ways in which we have tried to overcome these challenges. Here we address the issues of language/translation, voice and audience.

Language: Throughout our travels and our talks with women and girls in Lira, we have been challenged by conversations that have perhaps been as much as 50% Leblango. Many of the recordings we have used to provide the voices of the women have included Leblango translated into English. As researchers have noted, loss of a language also results in loss of aspects of the culture (Temple and Young 2004). Thus, as much as we attempt to offer the voices of Lira women, we must note the limitation that English places on their narrations. It is, for them, a colonial language that limits ways in which they can express their stories. Anyone who is bilingual can acknowledge ways in which one language can limit the expression of another. As such, we note ways in which language creates limitations in this project. We also recognise ways in which English, as an oppressive colonial language that has come to be recognised as "superior" can delimit the information we wish to provide for our readers.

Power and Privilege of the First/Third World: Power and privilege are typically a result of unearned status based on categories such as colour, economics and context. If not born into this category, a complex mix of variables, also not necessarily traits one can achieve, contribute to the likelihood of moving up the socioeconomic ladder. For example, I (Jody) was born into a family of low middle-class status and education. However, because of my race, my intelligence was recognised and promoted more than would be likely for a student of equal intelligence but from a non-White race. The same is true of Julia, born of British and Canadian White status. As much as we may long to wipe away this racial demarcation, we cannot. And, so, we are left determining ways in which we can use this unearned privilege to support those we see as equals, people designated as "two-thirds world" people, to have a voice as powerful as anything we might try to project.

Ultimately, we have made choices based on agreements with our colleagues and friends in Lira, who have chosen the limitations of English over not being heard at all. We have chosen to recognise these language issues as barriers to expressing the full stories of the women of Lira. We have recognised that our time over four years of visiting Lira is insufficient for creating a full story about what citizens experienced. We note difference in how we, the editors, tell our stories and publish real world narratives of our Lira participants. We recognise their stories, in spite of language issues and power differentials, to be the closest that we can get to present their life challenges to other parts of the world. Thus, we make this compromise in order for a larger population to understand and take a stand against the inhumanity that the women have faced for so many years and that other women will continue to face in the future if issues such as those described here are not addressed in a systemic way.

As we have traversed this landscape over several years, we have noted that more people have cell phones than flush toilets. As such, there is no going back on Western "progress." For better or worse, the people of two-thirds world areas see the work of the privileged one-third world as a way to improve their society and tell their stories. Recognising these contradictions, it is our desire to help our Northern Ugandan friends to make their lives known to the larger world.

Rhetorical Style: As editors and writers, we admit to having different styles of communicating. When reviewing the manuscript, Jody's husband Dick said that he could easily tell where Jody's words ended and Julia's began.

We struggled with this. Did we need to create a uniform voice? Were disparate voices appropriate? In the end, we decided that using our different voices was more authentic, given our different research that we believe informs one another's work. Julia is an art therapist and a registered mental health therapist. Jody holds a doctorate in educational studies, specialising in comparative and multicultural education. Of course, our voices are likely to be different. We view this as a strength rather than a weakness when we approach the work we document in this book, as it gives us a two-pronged understanding of Lira women's experiences. Yet, as we have chosen not to provide interpretations of Lira women's stories, these differences are not so important in most of the chapters.

We are also aware of juxtaposing an academic writing style with a more informal, descriptive style we sometimes choose as we describe our understandings of cultural underpinnings of the area. We are challenged by both our academic training, which tends to be exclusionary to a broad audience, but by which we feel bound in our professions; and the larger, more important desire to create a book for a broad public audience. We can only offer apologies for those lapses as we attempt to bridge academia with the important pursuit of informing the public at large.

2

Lira District, then and now

Kia Betty and Aceng Emma Okite

> We used to have music, dance and drama. Even over 400 people would come together. It built peace and unity. ~ Women's focus group, August 2011, Lira

As Emma is a historian and Betty works for the government, they were the perfect women to offer this chapter on the background of Lira and the Lango sub-region. What follows is their collaboration on this history.

Lira is home to the Langi people, whose native language is Leblango. The redistricting that occurred between 2005 and 2010 reduced the district from six counties down to four. According to a city population website (http://liradistrict.com/), a projected population for 2012 was four hundred and three thousand one hundred. Although the district escaped the first years of the LRA war, it was devastated in the last decade of the war, and the sub-region was the site of the largest massacre by LRA rebels at Barlonyo, which occurred in 2004. About one-quarter of the district population lives in the town of Lira, which is also the primary centre for commerce and government offices.

Joseph Kony's primary target was his own people, the Acholi. He claimed to want a new Uganda, one purified and populated by a new race of Acholi people. This was one reason that the Gulu region was most heavily affected, followed by Pader and Kitgum. However, he continued south and east into Lira and other districts in Uganda.

Before the war

Prior to the LRA War, Karamojong cattle rustlers from north-eastern Uganda caused Lira District's main disruption. The people of Lira kept cattle as a major source of wealth. Families cherished cattle as a source of income because milk, skins and even the cows could be sold as needed, with some of the income paying school fees for the children. Cattle are also popular for bride price. However, the Karamojong believed that cattle were to be kept only by them because, they said that God gave cattle to them as a blessing. The Karamojong considered cattle owners from other ethnic groups in northern Uganda to be wrongdoers. The father of Okite Eunice, co-author of Chapter Four, was murdered by the Karamojong as the rustlers stole her family's cattle. Aside from this conflict, the people of Lira were characterised as very loving, happy and welcoming. Children were for all people to love. Langi people were known as peace lovers who embrace all tribes with no discrimination or segregation regarding race or tribal sentiments. They were also known for their hard work and honesty (Odongo, Okello and Odongo 2012).

The oft-quoted African adage: "It takes a village to raise a child," was prevalent in pre-war Lira. In a group conversation, our friend Regina Betty Okwir said the following:

> A child was for everyone, everyone's concern. Whenever you see a child loitering along the road, you … send him to school. A child is a community child. And everyone wants that child to grow up and help the community. You worked and you got the money to buy produce and other things. The issue of death was not rampant. The issue of prostitutes and street kids wasn't there. People were living like brothers and sisters in the community.

Family life was valued, and evening story-telling around fire pits was a cherished tradition for bringing extended families together and for teaching children cultural values and beliefs, much like the Acholi tradition of the *Wang-oo*, an evening ritual of lessons and stories told around a fire pit. For instance, one story by an elder proclaimed: "If you walk at night, you will die or be eaten by wizards." Such tales were designed to instil discipline in the children, especially adolescents who might otherwise loiter on the roads at night and engage in early sexual behaviours. An elderly story-teller lamented that the imposition of the British school system and organised rooms with rows of desks and memorised curricula had done much to destroy the traditional northern Ugandan way of teaching children. In focus group discussions, women made the following comments about traditional teaching and learning:

> There is a traditional welcome and it was performed to bring the children into the community. Like eating traditional food, these performances would help to create a bond among the local people. Another thing, people used to tell their children stories around the fire. You make the fire in the evening; you gather the children; and tell them stories of how you used to hunt, maybe when you met a lion and all that, what you needed to do. How you were attacked by wild animals – these things were told around the fire to the children. In that way, you are training the children to be brave and be good members of the community. Women told the stories as well as men. The men used to tell the boy children, and then the ladies, the girl children. But these days, I think the war has taken up everything.
>
> We used to have music, dance and drama. Women used to perform, especially during the dry season, from November to March. When the rains came, people would be busy in their gardens. But during the dry season, people had little to do and that was the time when people had good relations with the community, so we had much music, dance and drama performed, one community after another, just to bring people together. We would have dances almost every week. Even over 400 people would come together. It built peace and unity.

Most people from Lira District were, and still are farmers, although most cultivate crops on a small-scale, mainly for home consumption. The most popular crops include millet, sweet potatoes, beans, cassava and maize. Some farmers grew cash crops such as cotton, sisal and tobacco to supplement their family income, but much was lost due to the war and the Karamojong cattle rustlers. The people of Lira District were also traders, although they would typically deal in small-scale businesses to supplement their other income. Although the residents' incomes were modest, hunger was not so pervasive.

Traditionally, the people of Lira District and the Lango as an ethnicity value their cultural beliefs, such as respecting their clan heads and leaders. Lango society is organised into clans, beginning with the *Awi otem* (head of the family lineage). Higher levels are not inherited, and they progress from the *Won paco* (head of homesteads) to the *Jan Jago* (assistant sub-chiefs), *Rwot* (clan chiefs), and *Awitong* (supreme clan chief). The *Won Nyaci* is the Paramount Chief of clans in the Lango sub-region, elected by the college of *Owitonge*. The current *Won Nyaci*, Yocam Odur Ebii, comes from the Atek Omwono Pel clan (Lango Agenda 2012). His duties are to lead all the other leaders. He solves conflicts, and his word is final.

The traditional role of women has been house-keeping and child-bearing. As the war escalated, however, the plight of women was highlighted as many of the young girls were abducted and forced into early marriages.

During the war

Unfortunately, the joy and happiest days of Lira District and the people of the Lango sub-region dwindled with the arrival of Kony's war. One can fail to find words to describe life during the insurgency. "Trauma" falls short; human beings were reduced to completely nothing. As one survivor observed:

> So many parents, including the children, during the war – the rebels could come and get children and get people in the market. And then

> they rounded up people in the market and started shooting them. They could even decide to kill everyone there. Certain times you would be captured and they would say to you, "Who is this one?" "This is my husband." .... They would force you to chop your husband or they would force your child to chop you into pieces. And if you refused, all of you would be killed. (Women's focus group, Lira 2009)

Women continued to be marginalised along with their children whose rights were constantly abused, their voices unheard. Traumatisation of women and girls occurred through rape and defilement. Some became pregnant with unwanted pregnancies; while others contracted the HIV/AIDS virus. Many endured abduction and life as child soldiers and "wives" in the bush. The most unfortunate ones were killed and never returned to see their parents. Their horrific experiences often remain unspoken. Those who tell their stories report events that defy one's worst nightmares, such as the following; recounted by a friend:

> Some people who were abducted were forced to eat their fellow human beings. People's heads were used as cooking stones and their bodies as meat. .... And sometimes, the children who were abducted were forced to carry very heavy loads on their heads. Sometimes they would give you a bag of sugar and you were a child of 15 years, and you had to walk a distance of, I don't know, more than 400 kilometres before you stopped, so some of them ended up dying. .... And you knew when you did something they did not like, they would beat you, they would tie you up, even upside down. ... Many children also died of hunger. You would see a child lying there, and you would think he was alive. He'd be gone. So many children were ages of 8 to 12. Many of them died in the bush.

The memories of these tragedies still linger fresh in the minds of the Lango people. One of the biggest challenges during and post-war was accepting the children fathered by the rebels when they returned from the bush with their mothers and absorbing them within the communities. Peers who escaped abduction shamed returned girls for being raped and kept, even though these atrocities were through no fault of their own. With extensive counselling, psychosocial support, and rehabilitation, the girls and their children are slowly being accepted and reintegrated back into their communities and villages.

During the insurgency, most people in the district fled their homes because they feared abduction or death by the LRA. Some took refuge either in town or trading centres. Those who had relatives outside of the districts affected by the war fled there for safety, while those who had money bought land in secure and peaceful areas like Masindi, Hoima and Bweyale. The majority had to take refuge in protected camps called Internally Displaced Persons' (IDP) camps. By 2003, 90% of the war-affected population was living in IDP camps, with the majority under the age of twenty-five (Women's Commission 2004). Sixty-one of these camps were established in the Lango sub-region during the war years, with forty-seven thousand Lira District citizens taking shelter in them. Graft and inadequate food, healthcare, water, sanitation and education were widespread in these camps. Although there was supposed to be military security, the LRA still raided the camps, especially at nightfall, killing residents, abducting children, and setting huts on fire. Even the Uganda People's Defence Forces (UPDF) and Local Defence Units (LDUs) recruited youth under the age of 18 to be fighters (Women's Commission 2004). Although the last IDP camp in the region was officially closed in 2008, some people still live in the remaining huts.

Girls and women who took refuge in IDP camps changed their behaviours as a result of trauma and as a means to survive. Some took work as housekeepers to have some economic means. Moral corruption increased, as there was no privacy in camps; so, there was little division and respect between adults and children. A large number of women and young girls started trading in sex with the soldiers who were protecting the camps in exchange for a kilo of beans or a cup of *posho* (maize flour). As a result, HIV/

AIDS infections increased – becoming a time bomb that exploded when people went back home. The Lango sub-region has a high percentage of HIV infection, especially among women of married couples (TASO 2012).

Villagers who remained in their homes, and some families in IDP camps, began sending their children into the town centres in the hope that they would be better protected from the LRA. Night commuters, as they were called, left their homes by the thousands in the early evening and walked between 2-10 kilometres to town centres in order to sleep in makeshift shelters under lamp posts, near hospitals, bus parks, municipal buildings, and in other places that seemed less susceptible to LRA ambushes. During these walks, and while sleeping at night, girls were frequently the subject of sexual harassment and abuse. The Women's Commission (2004) reported girls disclosing sexual abuse, rape, and exploitation, exposing them to additional trauma as well as HIV/AIDS and early pregnancy (p. 3). A boy quoted in the report stated:

> I know of older boys that menace and rape girls as they come into town. I don't agree with what they do, but I do understand that they feel lots of pressure to meet girls. We used to have places we could go and talk to girls we found pretty. Eventually we would go to their parents asking if it was okay to marry their daughter. Those traditional places and customs are gone now. The war has made it very difficult to interact with girls. (pp. 10-11)

Married men with families lost hope for the future since they could not support their families in the camps, with the result that many families separated and divorced. The increase of broken homes left children with unstable support – forcing many to survive as street children. Young men of marital age were, and still are, impoverished and unable to afford a bride price. This has resulted in increased sexual activity outside of marriage and reduced respect for women.

Post-war

There has never been a formal peace treaty signed between Joseph Kony and the Ugandan government. However, between 2006 and 2007, rebels dispersed from the region. Lira started to recover, although the earlier village lives that people used to enjoy are unlikely to return, because of the common traumatic experiences of the inhabitants. Slowly, people began returning to their homes, although some refused. Attempts to return to property remain fraught with difficulties, as locating the original boundaries of one's land and where the homestead used to be is nearly impossible, since the rebels completely demolished housing structures. Furthermore, adults who could have shown returnees their original homestead locations and boundaries were either abducted, killed by rebels, or died from numerous illnesses contracted in the camps during the war.

Land wrangling became the order of the day in Lira District and Lango sub-region as a whole. To date, people are killing one another over land; an example is the killing in Atira, where a retired post office worker, named Muzee Oluge, was killed in August 2012. The loss of morality is intensified by alcohol abuse among traumatised villagers.

Poverty levels have drastically increased, and parents cannot support their children's school fees. Although this is obvious at primary and more so at secondary schooling levels, it is especially problematic in higher education. Post-war poverty has caused parents to return to their original traditional belief of supporting only boy-children at school and forcing girls into early marriage. When parents can marry off girls at early ages, they no longer need to provide for their education or welfare. Such beliefs have, however, caused some NGOs to renew support for girls' education. Examples include the Forum for African Women's Educationalists (FAWE) and Beadforlife, among others in Uganda.

Educational achievement needs improvement. The Uwezo 2011 assessment report found that governments in East Africa are focusing more on access than quality of education. Overall findings indicated that children do better when their parents visit their schools and talk about learning, and that "children whose mothers are educated perform better at English reading and mathematics" (Uwezo, 2011, p. 3). However, the assessment also found that too many children in the lower primary grades struggle with basic English and maths skills:

- 9 out of every 10 children in P3 could not read and understand an English story text of P2 difficulty level; and
- 7 out of every 10 children in P3 could not solve numerical written division sums of P2 level difficulty correctly (p. 3)

These statistics were for all of Uganda. However, in Lira, only 8 out of 100 children in Primary Three (P3) can read and comprehend a Primary Two (P2) English story, and only 12 in 100 P3 pupils can solve P2 level division sums (p. 52). There is great need for more teacher training, parent involvement, and women's education to increase the level of student academic performance.

As previously described, village life has presented challenges for rehabilitation, due to war trauma. Still, the Langi long to return to a peaceful existence and a return to family life and property, as exemplified by the 2012 Lango Conference in Lira, during which the *Te Kwaro Me Lango* Development Agenda was discussed by representatives of the Lango communities. Several provisions must be organised for peace to be permanent. The majority of people in Lira District and the Lango sub-region need to be rehabilitated through counselling and psychosocial support by professional counsellors. The citizens must rise above current poverty levels. For this to occur, women must be recognised as equal partners in Ugandan society; allowed to hold positions of leadership and power and to participate in politics at all levels. Although hope is slowly building, Lira youth are challenged to compete for national jobs, and most parents cannot afford enrolment at universities.

Although the physical war is over, there is still a psychological war, and it is manifested in people's behaviours. Post Traumatic Stress Disorders (PTSD) abound, and horrific tragedies remain fresh on people's minds because of the years of atrocities witnessed during the war. There is still much recovery and reconstruction needed in Lira District and Lango sub-region as a whole to heal the feelings, visions and images of the people towards themselves and others. In particular, girls need to be encouraged to register and stay at school until completion. Those who have dropped out of school must be encouraged to come back and complete school. And more, educational trainings for both teachers and parents must aim to increase student comprehension of academic subjects. Following chapters in this book will provide a window into programmes that are trying to do just that: provide information to parents in order to help them understand the importance of girls' education, and community organisations trying to help them with funding opportunities.

In 2007, UNICEF's report on the state of the world's children focused on the importance of educating girls. When girls and women are supported, educated and empowered, transformation occurs economically, socially, financially and politically, from the family to the larger society. In Uganda, women are the backbone of the country's economy, despite the patriarchal systems that make them and their children a little more than the property of their husbands. About 80% of the women in northern Uganda spend most of their time in their gardens growing food for their families to eat, along with the daily duties of cooking, cleaning and caring for their children and husbands. A supportive approach by both genders could allow women more time to both educate themselves and be involved in their children's education, with a result of improved education and abilities of children.

3

Concerned Parents Association

Ogwal Consy and Acen Eunice

Initially, the rebels started giving her girls one by one. One by one. One by one by one, but my daughter was not among them. ~ Consy

On Labour Day weekend, nestled safely within the brick walls of my new home in Boston, I turned on the MP3 audio recording of Jody and Emma's latest meeting with Consy, taking place in July 2013. I knew I would need to make special time to listen carefully to Consy's words, while trying not to focus on my emotions of being a concerned parent for my children many miles away. Even with grown-up children, a parent never gives up the feeling of wanting to protect them and only wants the best for them that life has to give. The terror of losing a child to rebel attacks and feeling disempowered to do anything is a dark pain that few could endure.

Nine years after her daughter's escape from the rebels, Ogwal Consy was able to recount the terrifying years that remain embedded in her heart and soul. Her particular story has a relatively happy ending, since her child, Acan Grace, returned from the bush and successfully pursued her education. Grace managed to escape with her baby daughter eight years after being abducted by the LRA rebels. Consy's faith kept her going during the nightmare of not knowing whether or not Grace was alive or would ever return. This story is universal in a group of parents who steadfastly looked out for each other as they each deeply suffered the pain of not knowing where their girls were, if they were suffering, or even if they were alive. Consy and her husband, Richard, were two leaders of the Concerned Parents Association, formed after the abduction of one hundred and thirty-nine girls from St Mary's School for Girls, in Aboke, Uganda. Thanks to the fearlessness of Sister Rachele, the headmistress at the school, and a young teacher named John Bosco Ocen, who followed the rebels' and girls' tracks through minefields and begged for the girls' return, one hundred and nine of the students were returned immediately. However, thirty girls were kept, Grace among them. Five of the girls died in captivity. The last return occurred in 2009, having been kept for thirteen years. The trials of their abductions have been recorded in the books *Aboke Girls: Children Abducted in Northern Uganda* (de Temmerman 1995) and *Stolen Angels* (Cook 2007), but the voices of their parents have been largely silent. This chapter begins with the story of Acen Eunice. Two step-sisters for whom she had become like a mother were abducted from St Mary's School for Girls, in Aboke. Next, Ogwal Consy, who overcame her fear and anger to search for her abducted daughter, relates her experiences. As women experience the labour of childbirth, the inherent labour of love lasts a lifetime.

Eunice

My name is Acen Eunice. I am thirty-six years old. I grew up in a very happy family with a humble background. Along my way, when I was in Primary Four (P4), I lost my biological father. I lost him to the Karamojong, the people who came to raid our cattle. They killed him. Immediately, Uncle Ben Pere, took me over as well as my brothers and sisters. He took care of all of us, as well as his own children. Along the way, some of my siblings, especially my step-brothers and sisters, dropped out of school and married. Most of the children from my mother's house went along with their education. But, on my step-mother's side, they were not so much involved in academics;

so, they branched into other directions, although at least one went a little bit further to Senior Four (S4).

I think my uncle used to like me more than the rest of the children, and he made life better. I went to school from primary 4 up to diploma level. I went to St Katherine Senior Secondary School and then to National Teachers College Ngetta where I trained as a secondary school teacher. When I finished my course, I started teaching. During these years, I also became like a mother to all of the children in my uncle's home.

In 1996, two of my step-sisters were at St Mary's School for Girls, in Aboke. They were abducted from there. We had recently visited them, and we were debating whether we should go back and see them since it was Independence Day. So, we decided it was okay to wait for the next visitation. But that night of Independence, the rebels came and took them. They were among the thirty girls that were kept behind after the release of 109 abductees. Their names were Ejang Susan escaped in 2004 and Alobo Jacqui. So, after that, their father worked together with the help of other parents. Consy was one of the parents whose daughters were taken captive. My Uncle Ben headed the parents' group. He became the first Executive Director of the Concerned Parents Association until he died in 1998. He went for a meeting in Kampala; and then started shivering in the meeting room. He was rushed to a hospital, and then we were told that he needed to be in a quiet place. Some good Samaritan brought him from Kampala back to his home in Lira. Then he was taken to the dispensary. His condition was worse and the next day, he was rushed to hospital. He stayed there for two days and then died. He did not talk to anyone. He died in the struggle for the release of the Aboke girls and other children who were abducted from northern Uganda, and he did not see any of the thirty Aboke girls come back.

So, I lost my uncle, and I took up the responsibility to care for the children. We had a troublesome auntie who wanted to take over the home and sell it; so, we ended up in court. Fortunately, the clan members supported me. I won the case. We have the home now. Thanks to God, the children started coming back in 2003.

Those who were in the bush are also back. At the time of writing this chapter, one is in second year, and another one is in first year of university. So, I struggled with family issues and I could not go on with my education anymore. I worked with the Concerned Parents Association at the Reception Centre, where we used to go and collect children from the military barracks, where they were often brought when they escaped from the rebels. We kept them at the reception centre; traced their family background, and recorded their abduction history. We reunited them with their families and also prepared the family to receive their child. This was hard work.

While I worked for the CPA, whenever I received children from the barracks, the first thing on my mind was, 'how are my sisters in the bush?' At the centre, many had lost their limbs. So many terrible things had happened. We had to assist some of the returnees and rush them to the hospital for medication.

I got used to this experience slowly-slowly. I worked there for six months and then I had to go and stay home. I had to help the children still at home, since I had become the head of the family. I struggled then, and now they are somewhere. I no longer provide most of their needs, apart from a few I am able to provide. I am unable to pay for their school fees. At the level of university, I cannot afford pay because I do not have income to push them ahead.

So, that has been my life over these years. During that time, we also lost our grandmother. She would cry for her grandchildren and for her son who died in the process of looking for the children she never saw again. The old woman cried almost everyday. To lose her child, and not to know the whereabouts of her grand daughters was too much for her. Besides, the rebels killed about sixteen people near our home and we had to ran to town. Two weeks later, our grandmother died in the hospital. We took her body back home for burial. This was how the war affected our family. And now I am trying to come out of it. But it is hard.

I stayed at home a year before I joined the National Rescue Committee. I worked there for six years, dealing with returned children. I met the same challenges I had at the Concerned Parents Association (CPA). Sometimes, I ended up giving half my earnings to the children. For example, I used my money to buy them school uniform and also provide them support. I am happy that helped so many children to survive.

It was a hard time for my family and me, because I was worried about my sisters and disturbed by my aunt's attempt to grab the family land. But thank God, we managed to overcome the problems.

Now I am a happy woman. I am happy there are so many children who recognise me. The children I taught at school, come to me and say: "You taught me in this course; do you remember you helped me in such and such a school? I benefited from your projects." So that is what makes me happier. I just pray that that the LRA situation will never come back.

You know, this is the first time I have spoken of my experience. I have never told this story to my family. Never! I am always there for them. When I go back to my own story, I cannot really believe it is me. But one good thing is that people like me. I also like people in the community and the orphans and all of the children. It is good when one has one's parents alive. But along the way, I also lost my mother. Three weeks after losing my mother, I also lost my brother who was in Senior Six. And as I have mentioned, I lost my father. Those were bitter times. My uncle took care of me, then died and left me with a family to take care of.

People often wonder: "This woman has been working, but she has nothing. She has not bought even a bicycle." But, I know I have done a lot. I will struggle to be someone in the future, God willing.

Consy

I am called Ogwal Consy. I am fifty-three years old, and I have six children. In my family, I was the sixth born. My mother had several miscarriages but two boys and four girls survived.

My parents were poor. My father was a peasant. When I reached Senior Two, he said: "Girls need to get married." And he said I should go and get married so as to give a chance to the other young ones. So, I was forced to get married after Senior two and have persisted. I was about 18; it was in 1980. And then, I had my first child. But I really had a lot of problems in my marriage. In 1990, my husband left me. I went back to school to learn how to type. I did not want to stay idle. After completing the course, I was employed in Gulu. I worked with the social security department as a finance secretary for three years.

One time, thugs killed my neighbour. I went outside to see what was happening, and they shot at me. After that, I reconciled with my husband.

I remember, October 9th, 1996, the Ugandan Independence Day, when I was watching the football match on TV and excited because my team was winning. My husband had left early in the morning to go to work, and came back at 8:30 p.m. I heard the sound of his motorcycle while at my neighbour's house. I was taking tea with bitter lemon when one of my children burst inside. My husband had sent him to pick me and take me home immediately.

As I entered our home, my husband told me that our daughter, Grace, had been abducted by Kony's army. I started to cry hysterically. I could not believe what he was saying. We ran to another neighbour, a reverend, and asked if he had heard the news of our daughter. We all left for the school. We wanted to follow the rebels and bring back our girls. It was a rainy night and others shouted at us not to go over the bridge, because we could fall into the water and get killed. We did not care; we wanted to follow the path the rebels had taken with our girls. We were told that the girls had been dragged from their dormitories at the school in the middle of the night.

One of the parents, a father, started to cry. It was the first time I saw a man cry. "What can we do?" we all cried out. We wanted to continue and pursue the rebels. Instead, we were told to remain at the school—it was too dangerous and we did not know where to go. Some parents tried to continue in their vehicles. We waited at the school until noon the next day. Some of the girls, I think eight of them, had escaped. They came back along the road, exhausted, frightened, with their legs swollen. They were so traumatised that they could not speak.

"What can we do?" we again cried out. Sister Rachele came back later in the evening and told us how she had followed the trail of the girls and caught up with Kony's army to demand the release of the girls. Initially the rebels started by giving her the girls, one by one until Sister Rachele demanded for all of them. The rebel commander lined up the 139 girls that ha been abducted and chose the beautiful ones he would keep. When Sister Rachele again demanded to have all of them, he retorted that she should be contented with the ones he was giving her or else they would all be taken away.

Meanwhile, my husband told me that he would continue to look for the girls. I was numb. I did not want to lose him, too. I went with one of the parents to see the girls who had returned but my daughter was not among them. I collapsed. A priest friend told me that I should join other women in prayer. When the last of the escaped girls arrived and Grace was nowhere to be seen, I againm collapsed. I could not move. "I'm going to die," I thought. The priest counselled me not to give up hope that Grace would come back. "Mama, pray," he told me. I could not hold back my tears. They started rolling down my face. I went home crying. "When would I see my child again?" I wondered.

Soon after the abductions, parents of the girls banded together and we formed the Concerned Parents Association (CPA). We also encouraged parents from nearby, whose children had also been kidnapped, to join us. With growing numbers, we could do more to demand government intervention to help us get our children back and also rehabilitate them. We could work together to prepare the communities to welcome the children back, even though they had committed terrible crimes and many had been forced to kill. We explained that the children were forced to commit crimes against their will, and that they would have been tortured and killed if they had not obeyed the command. We also came together to pray for peace and for the grace to forgive.

For two years, I waited. I got used to hearing vehicles that would come down the road, returning abducted girls. People tried to console me with news that Kony's army had stopped killing the girls and had chosen to keep many of them for wives of the commanders. "But what can we do?" parents continued to cry out. That was when we went international and told the government and anyone who would listen, that we had a list of names of the missing girls and we needed help. We had no money. The UN had initially offered some support, but did not follow through. We learned of three children who were in the bush. One came back when the commander who had forced her into marriage died. The other two were told that if they let anybody know of the commander's death, they would be killed. Eventually, Kony killed the girls.

There were many struggles. In 2000, IDP camps were established. The army told us not to use guns, or the children would certainly die. A group of government soldiers tried to rescue the girls, but there was a gunfight and many of the soldiers were killed. Some of the girls were also killed by stray bullets from the government troops. One girl, Judith, an Aboke girl, was subsequently tortured and beaten to death to show the abducted children what would happen if anyone betrayed Kony and tried to leave. "If you want to be alive, don't tell, don't move, or you will die!"

Sister Rachele, determined to find all the girls she had to leave behind, kept searching and putting her life in danger, over and over again. Reviving the search in 2002, the Concerned Parents Association visited the IDP camps and military barracks to get information. After various government troop encounters with Kony's army, one by one, the girls began to come back. It was now 2003, and finally God started making miracles. One by one, the girls returned but my daughter was not among them.

In one of the military attacks in Sudan, Ugandan soldiers found a two-year old abandoned child. Richard and I quickly drove to the Ugandan commander's reception centre to get the news. The child was found without the mother. We suspected its mother was one of our girls, and we thought that maybe someone had seen her. Eunice's sisters, Susan and Jacqui, had told us of seeing Grace in Sudan, so we hoped this event might lead us to her. Instead, the commander brought in a chair for me to sit on and told me that Grace had been killed on 13th July. As my husband and I looked at each other, I felt dead. But I said: "Let us keep on praying." That was on the 8th of August. I went without food on the 8th, 9th, 10th. On the last day, I talked to God. I said: "God, I will not sleep until I find this child." I cried and said: "I want this child." And he finally answered. He made it happen.

Apparently there had been an attack and one of Kony's officers, Kenneth Banya, was injured in a bomb explosion. His wife, Grace, was sitting under a tree when the bomb went off. Her son was with her, and her son's body was the only one found, which possibly meant our daughter's body was still in the bush. At first, we thought it was another Aboke girl, Janet's baby. The government commander wanted me to look at the rebel photos to see if I could identify the body of Grace. "Where is the body?" I demanded to see proof. "Show me the photos!" I was shaken and collapsing and I could not look. But Grace was not there in the photos.

Banya was captured in 2004. I went to the barracks to see him to ask if he had seen Grace. On July 17th, he told me to keep quiet. He was the father of the two-year old child and Grace was the mother. "Don't talk nonsense!" I cried. I sent her to school, not to be married. The man was shaking, obviously frightened by his capture. I cried hysterically. When I settled down, I learned that he was trained as a pilot in Russia and had been forced into Kony's army. I wanted to go into the bush to rescue my daughter. Sister Rachele consoled me not to cry. Grace had delivered a second child. Sister Rachele believed the rebels would not kill Grace, as she was the mother of two of their children. We learned this update on August 1st. The rebels kept moving into Sudan. Grace was with them.

In June and July of 2004, two other abducted girls escaped, Rebecca and Jenna. "Why not *my* child?" I yelled at God. So I waited. Thursday, Friday—until Wednesday of the following week when I went overnight with a neighbour to pray at the church. I decided to talk with God from 8pm to 6am. I did not sleep. Instead, I asked God: "Please, open the door to let her come back. God, I am not going to ask anymore."

Sunday, Monday, Tuesday passed. The mother of Jenna came. We learned in the newspaper that the wife of Banya escaped during an attack on the rebels. In the attack, two of the rebels, one in front of Grace and that one behind had been killed, and the Grace, along with several others, ran for safety from gunfire and exploding bombs. The others remained for a while, but because Grace's baby would not stop crying, the girls abandoned her, fearing that the baby's cry would let others know their hiding spot and they would get killed. After a day, Grace started looking for the other girls in vain. Her baby was hungry and would not stop crying. Grace searched for food and stumbled across someone's home in the bush. She scrambled around in the abandoned house, desperate for food. She slept for the first time in a long time with her baby under a tree. Three, four, then five days passed, and Grace became scared of having no food. She found seven mushrooms, picked them, roasted and reserved them.

On the sixth day, she stared a lion in the face, not knowing her fate. They both looked at each other and then the lion left. She then decided that indeed no one was coming for her and she needed to find her way out of the valley. Grace moved back to the abandoned house and was startled by the man who owned it. She told him that she had been abducted and was scared and wanted to go home. The man was terrified that Kony's army would return and arrest or kill him. He said if he was killed it would be Grace's responsibility. "I just want to get home," she said. "Let's pray that they don't find us on the way," he said. The man then took Grace to the Ugandan soldiers.

Grace took the little she had and the mushrooms she had prepared. Kony's army had told the abducted children that if they dared surrender to the Ugandan forces, they would immediately be tortured and raped. So, she lied to the government commander about who she was, afraid of being tortured. "No," he said, "We have a list. You are an Aboke girl. We will give you a good welcome." The soldiers gave her a new T-shirt and took her and the baby to Gulu. By Tuesday, she had reached the local barracks and we read in the newspaper that one more girl had been found. My husband was in Gulu at the time on business. So, he went to the barracks and reunited with Grace. I was overjoyed when he brought her back home. For eight years I had a broken heart, but I never gave up.

* * *

It is important to note that thousands of other children were abducted; and in most cases, their fates have not been as positive as those of the rehabilitated Aboke girls. Okula (2013) says the Concerned Parents Association provided an international voice for the girls; and numerous scholarships have been offered to them but not availed to other returnees. Okula discusses this not as a criticism of the CPA, but rather as a way of demonstrating the power that a group of concerned citizens can manifest.

4

Women of Lira

Kia Betty and Aceng Emma Okite

> I have hope because awareness and action are rising for women's rights. A belief is growing that enough is enough. But I am outraged because women and girls continue to suffer high levels of discrimination, violence, and exclusion. They are routinely blamed and made to feel shame for the violence committed against them, and they too often search in vain for justice. Michele Bachelet, UN Women Executive Director, International Women's Day, 2013

In 1975, The United Nations proclaimed March 8th International Women's Day to recognise women's achievements regardless of national, ethnic, linguistic, cultural, economic or political differences. It is an occasion for looking back on past struggles and accomplishments and to look ahead to the untapped potentials and opportunities that await future generations of women. In Uganda, this day is set aside as a national celebration. In Lira, crowds of people gather in the main square, with marches by school children, speeches, dance and festivities. Behind these joyful demonstrations, though, women also gather to discuss on-going issues of abuse and oppression, and they consider ways to slowly change their communities to become more equitable and safe spaces for women. This day, one day a year, represents what every day ought to be in Lira: respecting and honouring the ways in which women can improve the social, psychological, and economic aspects of society. There is much to do in order for this respect to become a reality.

This chapter is in two parts. The first section, by Betty Kia, explains the role of rural women in the district. Part Two, by Aceng Emma Okite, describes many of those women who have risen to leadership roles and how they are trying to change their community and country. We recognise that the addition of names in current positions can "date" a book. However, we believe it important to publicly acknowledge and honour women who have broken down gender barriers; and we ask forgiveness of the many not named here, who are also committed to the struggle so that future generations of girls will have more freedoms and opportunities.

Part One: The State of Rural Women in Lira

By Betty Kia

The purpose of this section is to consider the true state of most women in the rural community based on my personal experiences working in the rural areas for over seven years, dealing mostly with issues affecting women. I hope to provide a clear reflection of what most women in the community experience as well as a number of recommendations that call on all stakeholders to take action to improve the status of our women and girls. Women compose a larger number of the rural community than men. They play a great role in the economic development of their families, community and the nation at large. It is time to recognise their worth and dignity.

Over the years, I have noted that most researchers restrict their interviews to the urban areas, making for an incomplete picture of women's issues and status in Lira. Many urban women do not fully realise what takes place in the rural community. Poverty, high levels of illiteracy, cruel treatment by their spouses, and denial of the right to property characterise rural women's lives. Women spend most of their time in gardens and business places attempting to feed their families and to make small amounts of money (about the equivalent of one US dollar a day) for additional necessities, in addition to caring for their children and their homes. During farming seasons, women spend most time in fields raising crops such as cassava, beans, maize, millet, simsim and groundnuts. Sadly, at the same time, the women are farming and tending to chores, many men can be found in drinking places throughout the day and evenings. In their study of displaced persons in northern Uganda, Roberts and his colleagues (2011, p. 872) found that 33.4% of men had an alcohol disorder, compared to 7.1% of women, and that men were "7 times more likely than women" to be above the threshold for alcohol disorder. Despite their efforts, women are victims of nearly epidemic levels of domestic violence.

In spite of their circumstances, women own nothing in their homes. All the property, including the children, belongs to the men (Dolan 2003). When a husband dies, in-laws may send away the widows without any possessions or money. The worth and dignity of women are not recognised in the community; in other words, they are little more than "property" of men.

Girls must help their mothers with work and childcare. Their education is typically neglected in the family. Even the few who enrol in schools frequently drop out at the primary level because parents fail to raise sufficient school fees, and the priority goes to boys' education. If registered in primary, most girls do not attend the second term, because they must help their mothers in the fields. Because bride price goes to the girls' parents, too many are forced into early marriages (McCormac and Benjamin 2008). I will describe these issues in detail in the sections below.

Illiteracy

Because so few girls attend school, most women in the rural communities are not literate. In an interview with a few women in a rural community, I realised that most of the women regret that their parents never sent them to school. There are some who are willing to join adult education programmes, even beginning at a primary level. These women, however, are challenged by overwhelming family responsibilities. As a result, their education moves along slowly, and many do not complete the studies.

During a visit to one of the villages, I spoke with a woman named Santa who actually returned to a school in Lira and began at Senior One level at St Katherine School. She supported herself by becoming a board member at the school and through tailoring. She had the vision of becoming a councillor at the district level. After graduating from St Katherine, she attended All Saints University Lango and earned a diploma in social sciences. She registered at the secondary school when she was 32 years old, completed after four years, graduated from All Saints, and is now a councillor at the district. Her example can be a great encouragement to fellow women. Myself, I am sub-county chief of Awei in Alebtong District, and I settle cases of domestic violence, child abuse, rape, drunkenness, defilement, separation and divorce, and land disputes, among others. I volunteer for Women Achievers, which encourages young girls to stay at school and older women to return to school. We hold sessions in rural villages to explain to parents the benefits of sending their daughters to school.

Inequalities

As mentioned above, the education of girls is not valued yet in the rural communities. Girls are viewed as a source of labour and income for the family. They are expected to help their mothers with domestic work such as washing, cooking, fetching water, weeding, and taking care of the younger children at home while the mothers are away. Therefore, even with Universal Primary Education (UPE), their attendance in schools is sporadic, resulting in poor performance. As a result, the girls become discouraged and believe that they cannot succeed in school. Additionally, some boys at school sexually assault or threaten girl students, and some male teachers promise good grades in exchange for sexual favours (McCormac and Benjamin 2008). Fears of assault, rape, or unwanted pregnancies cause some girls to drop out of school – and some parents to insist that their daughters quit. These same fears cause parents to marry their girls off at young ages, hoping that if they do this early enough, their daughters will not have a chance to be raped, become pregnant, or be shamed by the community. Girls who are not attending school may also be forced into early marriage to bring a bride price for the family. Older people must come to recognise that a girl child, just like any other person, has the right to be respected. Prosecuting perpetrators of sexual assaults would help to bring about this recognition.

Rural girls in Lango face the issue of sexual abuse both inside and outside of school. For example, older men with money, clothes, phones and other enticements may lure them into having sex. This common experience exposes the girls to early pregnancy and sexually transmitted diseases, including HIV/AIDS, which often results in damaging the life and future of the girls, as they are disgraced and often sent from their homes. Local leaders must become vigilant and report such cases to relevant authorities for further action.

There is great need for parents to encourage and support their daughters to stay in school, and to make school safe for girls. Such needs, however, uncover more gender prejudice. In some of the sub-counties in Lira, women described strong resistance from their husbands regarding the promotion of girls' education. The men tend to support early marriage of the girls more than their education. A woman stated: "Men are more reluctant on the education of the girls as compared to the boys, and yet as mothers we do not have any source of income to send the girls to school." Another mother remarked: "To help the girls better, there is need to convince the fathers so that they can come to understand and value the education of a girl child and send them to school." Without the support of the father, it is likely that their daughters will not receive an education. The men, therefore, need education about the importance of girls' education. If men and women work together as a family, along with various government programmes towards poverty eradication in the district, they will be in a better position to support and send their girls to school. The principle is "fight poverty, educate the girl child."

Domestic violence

The problem of domestic violence inflicted on women and children is rampant in both urban areas and rural communities, despite attempts by the state and non-governmental organisations to protect them. In 2007, the Uganda Bureau of Statistics reported that 68% of women who were ever married between the ages of 15-49 had experienced domestic violence (US Department of State, 2008). Women rarely report abuse because they fear additional abuse, embarrassment, or poverty if they are thrown out of their home (US Department of State, 2008). Often, they are unaware of their rights or they do not know how to report abuse. Additionally, they are unlikely to gain a positive outcome, as many law enforcement officials consider a wife beating a husband's prerogative.

Unfortunately, abuse has become a norm in the community. In fact, there are common sayings that "a woman who is not beaten up by her husband is never happy," and "it's a sign of love for a woman to be beaten by the husband." The women have contributed to this situation by concluding: "I will suffer because of the children." Since children are "property" of their fathers, the women give themselves up to suffering abuse in order to raise their children. This calls for yet a greater action by the communities to improve the situation of women. Clearly, local authorities need to enforce laws so that women are respected and their rights valued in the community. Beating women does not resolve conflict, nor does it indicate a man's love. Love does not cause pain to another. Years of war have resulted in the use of violence as a form of communication, especially for men

(Dolan 2008). More community programmes to teach respectful communication could help men learn to talk and listen to women. Meanwhile, the state should enforce laws that protect the rights of women and girls in the country, and serious actions must be taken against those who inflict domestic violence. Currently, the victims are ignored and women left at the mercy of physical and psychological violence.

The situation, a fact of life encompassing so many rural women, makes is hard for them to participate in development programmes that encourage woman and promote discussion between the sexes. The violence in homes affects them physically, psychologically, and socially. When the home is not in peace, children end up leaving school out of stress, depression, or basic survival needs. And when parents divorce, girls remain to resume the responsibility of their mothers – rendering them unable to attend school.

Women's rights

Even though Uganda ratified the UN Convention on the Elimination of All Forms of Discrimination against Women (CEDAW) in 1985, we are far from understanding and accepting the concepts of women's rights and equality in the rural areas. In my interactions with rural people on this matter, I realise that these issues are a source of conflict in our communities. Neither men nor women understand the meaning of women's rights, resulting in tensions between them that sometimes end in home violence. In one of the villages in Lira, I learned that the men stopped allowing their wives to attend trainings on gender issues. One stated: "The issues of gender are making women big-headed." Some actually moved further from community centres to prevent the women from attending such meetings.

This situation calls for a deeper understanding about human rights in general. To dispel some of the anger raised about women's rights, it may benefit us to begin with community dialogues on the rights of all – men, women, and children – to first create a peaceful understanding about universal respect and human dignity. The current situation is likely to result in fewer women attending trainings, and continuing ignorance and oppression in the community.

Recommendations: What can be done to improve the lives of women and girls in the community?

Although problems are many, they must be systematically addressed to move towards positive change and development in the district. Most important, villagers need to hold pubic forums to discuss each major issue in detail.

Poverty

Poverty is a major challenge, as the war left the people more impoverished than they were prior to the insurrection. Buildings and homes were destroyed; schools and businesses were ransacked. Reconstruction requires capital. We still rely too much on international organisations and grants to sustain us. The goal must become self-sufficiency. One of the many paths is for Lango people to work together to own their own crops and businesses. Although international businesses can bring capital into the region, they can also weaken opportunities for individuals to increase their profits by purchasing raw materials for less than they are worth. As an example, there is a large foreign business in Lira that purchases raw cotton from individual farmers. On their own, the farmers cannot bargain for fair prices. However, if they worked together and formed a cooperative business, they could demand reasonable prices. As they gain capital, they could begin to process their own crops, strengthening the region and keeping money in the hands of the citizens. More money means more opportunity to pay school fees for all children. In public forums, men could learn the value of educating their daughters. Research overwhelmingly indicates that educated women are healthier; they raise healthy children; they insure for their children's education; and they contribute greatly to the economy (UNCEF 2007).

Illiteracy

Most of the rural women are illiterate, because they either never attended school or they received inadequate education. Because so many are past school age, adult literacy and education centres are critical needs, but they must be flexible enough to provide times when women can attend. Weekends, especially Sunday afternoons, could allow more women to attend. When women are literate, they are far less likely to be cheated in business ventures. Additionally, there are illiterate men who also require adult education so they can progress in business. Creating separate same-sex literacy classes would increase enrolment and completion because, as adults, each gender is unlikely to be comfortable in mixed classes: men, because they would want to be ahead of the women; and women, because succeeding in a mixed class could cause them discomfort, or even be threatening.

Early marriage and sexual/domestic abuse

These situations must be stopped, and they require serious consideration by the government of Uganda. Even though Uganda ratified CEDAW (unlike the US), it has no specific laws prohibiting domestic violence. In fact, in 2006, President Museveni declared that there was no need for a domestic violence bill (Takiwaa, 2007). The 2007 US Department of State report on Uganda stated that 60% of men and, surprisingly, 70% of women are accepting of wife beating (US 2008). When a majority of women find it acceptable to be beaten by their husbands, policy is unlikely to change.

Women in the community need to be fully educated to know and understand their rights, roles and responsibilities in society, and they must come to have self-respect before these practices will change. In addition, men must be educated to understand that the rights of women are not acts of violation against men. Rather, they are an important step to bring harmonsation between the sexes so they can work together to support and develop their families and community.

However, given the years of war that made violence common, this issue will not be quickly erased. Community-based organisations need to take a lead in building dialogues between men and women on this issue. Community drama might aid in forwarding such discussions. This topic must also be discussed extensively in schools, when boys must receive instruction on respecting girls and women, and on creating a healthy family life when they marry.

Child marriage in Uganda is at 46% (UNICEF 2012), above the average in African nations. Child brides are at a higher risk for complications or death during childbirth, incidence of HIV/AIDS, poverty, and domestic abuse (girlsnotbrides.org 2012). Parents must be educated to realise that a bride price is fleeting, while an educated daughter can bring about a lifetime of additional income. Marriage and sexual relations occurring when a girl is not fully developed can result in numerous risks, even death, during pregnancy. Encouraging girls to stay at school and advocating safe schools are important steps to reducing early marriage and pregnancy.

Education

Because girls are given less support by parents to attend school, we need to begin by educating parents about the importance of girls' education. The 2004 UNESCO *State of the World's Children* report specifically investigated the need for girls' education, but subsequent reports have also noted this importance (McCormac and Benjamin 2008). This research needs to be conveyed to parents so that they can realise the importance of educating their girls, both in terms of raising the economic potential of their region and country, but also in terms of helping them personally.

We can begin by organising special training workshops in schools for female teachers to help them connect with the girls in schools, as girls typically feel safer to share their problems with female teachers than with male teachers. We have female teachers who greatly encourage girls, help them with personal issues, and provide a support system to help maintain young girls in schools. Still, in Uganda, the majority of teachers are male. The creation of scholarships for girls who plan to become teachers could encourage more girls to go into that field. However, conditions for teachers must also improve in order to attract good candidates to that occupation. Current conditions for teachers, especially in the rural areas, are quite poor. They often go unpaid, or they may wait for several months to receive a small wage. Some teachers walk several miles each way to reach rural schools; so, they do not tend to be at the schools every day. There is inadequate housing for teachers near the rural schools, and many prefer to be in larger towns where there is more to do with their free time. The government must recognise and support the importance of regular and fair teacher pay.

Accommodations taken for granted in industrialised countries can make the difference between girls remaining in school or dropping out. Schools in Uganda need to create environments that encourage girls to stay at school. For instance, there must be separate toilets for the girls as they need privacy, especially once they reach puberty. When girls reach puberty, they tend to drop out of school in large numbers because they lack separate toilet facilities, and they become embarrassed or are teased by their male counterparts. Additionally, they require sanitary pads, preferably something highly absorbent that can be washed and reused to prevent more problems with respect to trash and recycling. Girls also require water to keep themselves clean during their menstrual cycles. Without these basic needs, girls are prone to drop out of school.

School administrators can organise dialogues for girl students, their mothers, female teachers, and women achievers to freely share their challenges and experiences, and to come up with concrete recommendations to improve their lives in society. Experiences of strong women leaders can encourage girls to stay at school and give them advice on future pathways for them. In addition, after forming a base of trust among the girls and women, it will be important to include men in these conversations. Agreement between the genders is essential in establishing respect for women leaders.

Violence against women, and women's rights

The government of Uganda must become more active in establishing policies and laws that protect women against domestic violence. And they must enforce laws already in place. Additionally, women themselves must organise to insist that current and new laws protect them from domestic violence. In collaboration with parents, teachers, NGOs and governmental agencies, women must insist on basic human rights that protect them against discrimination and abuse.

Part Two: Women Leaders

By Aceng Emma Okite

Gender bias in Ugandan society is rooted in the African concept of social order, buttressed by traditional spirituality. The marginalisation of women is taken for granted and argued forcefully on the platform of "our culture" and patriarchy. The power of a woman is measured by her reproductive capacity, and her access to resources is typically guarded by a male authority figure. Hence, women continue to struggle within oppressive social systems and government. Although education and empowerment have brought success for individual women, the position of women in the wider society is still lamentable. Women of Lira and the Lango sub-region are not an exception; they are still marginalised in the economic, professional, social, and political spheres of society, and their voices are undermined in decision-making.

Much needs to occur in Lira to increase the rights and capabilities of women. However, many strong women in Lira are working to attain gender equality, and some have managed to rise above the norm. As an example, many women are returning to complete their education after dropping out of school, often as a result of observing what women leaders are doing in their district. They are coming to understand that education is a basic human right and a key to empowerment for women and girls. Benefits through education have made some women of Lira District very strong and capable of helping their families and local societies as well as recommending global change.

What follows is a listing of remarkable women in Lira District.

Dr Aceng Jane Ochero, because of her hard work, was promoted from the position of medical superintendent, Lira Regional Referral Hospital to Director General, Uganda medical services, one of the biggest posts, held only by men in the past. She is a role model for girls who want to enter the medical profession. As a female doctor, she inspires girls and women through radio talk shows and on national television as she discusses health issues for girls, women and the country at large.

There are many women in the banking sector. The former Stanbic Bank manager, Achola Eunice, is one of the strong women in banking in Lira. Odongo Pamela, a manager of Diamond Trust Bank in Lira, is another prominent woman in banking in Lira district. The contribution and positions of these women in the banking sector has uplifted the women in Lira as well as girls' education. These women leaders frequently talk to girls at school workshops, and at picnics and crusades about aiming high in education and having positive views concerning their future.

Politically, Lira District has had several women elected to government positions. Amuge Rebecca Otengo was a former Member of Parliament who became both the Honourable Minister of State for Northern Uganda and Member of Parliament for Alebtong District, a sister district to Lira. Ongom Joy represents women of Lira in Parliament. Madam Ongom exemplifies the capability of women in high government positions. Within the Lira District local government are more women leaders; among them,

Madam Eyal Lillian, who is Deputy Chief Administrative Officer for Lira District. Madam Acen Jolly works as District Community Development Officer, and her work is to plan and mobilise the communities regarding development. One of the district councillors is Madam Santa Angela who represents the people of Adekokwok in the district local government. Achola Poly Pauline is the Assistant Chief Administrative Officer; Apio Esther, the Community Development Officer. Apio Lillian Ochari is the Chief of Dokolo; Betty Kia (one of the authors of this book) is the Chief of Alebtong, and Mrs Jane Frances Offungi is the Municipal Education Officer. Women in these positions of power demonstrate to girls that they, too, can attain important positions to help decide the future of their communities.

Other outstanding women are in the field of education, such as head teachers in schools. We have, for example, Mrs Dengai Betty, headmistress of a primary school. Madam Amongi Lydia is a teacher who owns her own primary private school called Mother Ida. Recently, she was promoted to District Education Officer for Dokolo District in Lango sub-region. Several women are also heading secondary schools, such as St Katherine's Secondary School for Girls, headed by Alambuya Connie. Lira Town College is a school that for a long time was headed by men only. Now, a woman, Acen Sophia Rose, heads the schools. Although past performance at Lira Town College was poor, the students are beginning to perform well and pass their courses. The Lango sub-region also claims at least two scholars at Makerere University: Florence Ebila, who lectures in Gender and Women's Studies; and Betty Ezati, the first female dean of the College of Education at Makerere.

Several women lead non-governmental organisations, such as Florence Auma Apuri who worked for many years with Action Aid International, which helps girl students and their parents. She continues with the work of advocating for and promoting women's rights at the United Nation's Population Fund (UNFPA). Others are co-authors of this book. Eunice Akwang directs Te-cwao that helps adults and children by providing adults with employment skills and children with educational opportunities. Okwir Betty Regina has created a community-based organisation called Women Achievers, which travels to rural areas with women leaders to encourage parents to send their girls to school. She has also founded a primary school for children who were previously too far from a school to attend classes. And I, Aceng Emma, am the founder and director of PsychoAid International. It is the first local psychological counselling centre in Lira District that caters to the general public.

In the business sector, we have prominent, outstanding women who have affected the lives of the people of Lira District for the better. Among them is Engola Betty, the wife of the Honourable Minister of Housing and Urban Development, Sam Engola. Mrs Engola is a very strong woman who has helped women and girls create businesses to sustain themselves. She has given some women financial support in the form of start-up capital for their businesses. She is also one of the brains behind the popular Lira Hotel. Her simple life and hard work have been a model for many women in Lira. Apio Vicky Stella represents women in the field of information technology. She owns a secretarial business and has used her work to encourage many young girls and women in Lira.

Although women in Lira District have begun to hold positions of power, more needs to be done so that women in these positions gain respect for their work. Many of their male counterparts see them as threats. Some of these women leaders receive no support from their husbands, and they are threatened with domestic violence. Thus, even though they hold positions of leadership, their self-esteem and physical wellbeing may suffer. They need more empowerment economically, educationally, and financially in order for the younger generation to see them as role models. Girls must be encouraged by all stakeholders, including parents, teachers, and the media, to participate in and learn about the social, economic and political functioning of society, to inspire them to take part in decision-making processes at all levels. And boys must learn that such empowerment is not a threat to their lives. Rather, it is an important means to bring stability and prosperity to the region.

Te-cwao Youth and Elderly Association

Eunice Akwang

"As women have gained more rights they are not looked at as underprivileged, useless people in the society, but as a class of people that deserves more respect." Eunice Akwang

Walking out of Lira town on the Kirombe East Boundary Road, one comes to a former IDP camp where several families still live. Next to it, one will find women and men weaving textiles, making baskets, and moulding colourful paper beads outside a small shop. They have come together as an association called Te-cwao Youth and Elderly Association (TYEA), founded by Omuka David in 2006. Te-cwao means "under the tree," named for the large, beautiful *shea* tree shading the land where the organisation is based.. TYEA's vision is "to have communities which are free from abject poverty," and its mission is "ensuring that vulnerable people, in particular, and all the communities, in general, in Lango sub-region, are sustainably enjoying better livelihoods in sustainable environments." At the time of writing the current article, in 2015, it has 70 members.

I met Eunice Akwang and her father David in 2011. The latter described the founding of Te-cwao; introduced us to members of the community-based organisation (CBO); and took us to see the nearby IDP camp. When Julia and I returned in 2013, the founder of

TYEA had just died, and Eunice was mourning his passing. She has struggled greatly since then, yet she has managed to keep his dream alive. Te-cwao continues to provide training to women and men in creating jewellery, weaving baskets and cloth, raising pigs, and thus providing members with an income. What follows is Eunice's story:

* * *

My name is Eunice Akwang, the third-born in a family of eight children. I am grateful that all of my brothers and sisters are alive, since many families lost members during the LRA war. Most of them have jobs or are still students. One of my brothers is in a seminary, in his fourth year of training to become a Roman Catholic priest. I am married, and I have two children, a five-year-old daughter and baby son.

I was a little girl when the LRA war intensified in early-2000. According to my memories and experiences, people used to live freely and stay as a family before the war. We lived happy lives. I remember parties were held when a new baby was born in a family, and every community member would be a part of the celebrations. The unity among people also was very strong, and we would be concerned about our neighbours.

There were very few school dropouts compared to the situation during and after the war. Most families lived above the poverty level. They could afford two meals a day and have their children in school, because farming was carried out on a larger scale before the war, and the majority of families owned cattle. The animals were sold and the money earned would be used for marriages and domestic needs. It is true that, according to tradition, girls were looked at as a source of wealth, as cattle were paid to her parents for a bride price. Before they were married, most girls would remain home to help in the domestic and farm work. As a result, boys had the highest chances for an education. But in 1996, the government announced the Universal Primary Education (UPE) programme, which increased girls' opportunities to be in school.

My father, David Omuka, was a lecturer at Mbale Polytechnic College, teaching Business Administration, Accounting, and Commerce. He was well liked by his students. After retiring from teaching in 2010, he became the auditor at St. Kizito Counselling Centre, where he worked until his death. I remember him participating in drama and in the church choir. He was a good singer. I was inspired by his hard work, determination and achievements.

Perhaps because of my father's love for education, I was lucky. At a time when many girls were not sent to school, I completed secondary school, even though my family had to move to a camp during the war. We lived in an IDP camp for three years. The schools in the camps were overcrowded, and most teachers were not committed to their teaching. I was not able to go to university. So, I ended up at a tertiary institution where I graduated with a diploma in Human Resource Management. I was fortunate to have that, as so many young people never finished secondary school. But my dream of reaching the university vanished.

In the camp, life was very difficult. Many girls were raped or otherwise defiled. As a result of the forced sex, many girls got pregnant and dropped out of school. Some were infected with HIV/AIDS, and some became child mothers. Because the camps were so overcrowded, many people had to sleep outside the tents, and there was no privacy. Sex was often public, and children were not respected, resulting in the sexual abuse of young girls. Very young children were also involved in child labour, as they often had to walk long distances carrying items such as pancakes and steamed maize as a means of survival.

After the war, there were so many orphans and widows as a result of the atrocities committed by the rebels against the people in the region for two decades. Children had lost their parents and women had lost their husbands, either through war casualties or disease, as health conditions in camps were often terrible. For children, this resulted in greatly decreased school attendance since they had no one to give them the support they needed. Besides, many parents took to drinking during and after the war. They used the little money they had for alcohol rather than school supplies and so kept their children at home. One of Te-cwao's beneficiaries, an orphan named James, says, "The world is so wild without parents. Nobody treats you like a child. You become a problem to everybody because of asking for assistance. What a world!"

Te-cwao Youth and Elderly Association is a registered CBO, founded at a time when the government received funding from the World Bank under the programme called Northern Uganda Social Action Fund (NUSAF) in 2006. The goal of NUSAF was to aid in restructuring northern Uganda towards the end of the LRA war. The Ugandan government used it to help with start-up funds for small organisations. Beginning with 35 members, Te-cwao received funding to begin a piggery project. Now, these funders no longer provide money. Like many others, TYEA receives no major outside funding and must rely on what it can find, including dues from members. We focus on sustainable projects.

Te-cwao was founded under the following aims and objectives:

- To reduce poverty and raise the living standards of its members, especially the widows, persons with disabilities, school dropouts, the elderly, orphans, and people living with HIV/AIDS and the surrounding community who would wish to join them;
- To improve the livelihood of the vulnerable through sensitisation, initiation and implementation of social and economical activities and the projects that would be initiated from those activities;
- To provide health services such as counselling on HIV/AIDS, prevention and care; and
- To provide members with cheap bio-gas for lighting and cooking that is cost-effective for low-income earners.

Te-cwao has strived and still struggles to change the lives of community members in the region through income-generating activities as mentioned earlier: weaving, textiles, making baskets, making paper beads jewellery and pig farming.

Success Stories

Although TYEA was founded in 2006, income-generating activities were not started until 2009 on a very small scale, with only five women and two men being trained in craft making. The first five women to be trained were Susan Amadi, Anam Teddy, Amooti Safina, Semmy Abongo and Amolo Enin. They remain committed to their work. These five women have also trained more than 35 people who are now members of the association in handicraft making.

There has been a big challenge in finding a market for the crafts, since many women and men are now involved in the trade, resulting in increased volume of production with no ready market. Fortunately, we have been able to open up a crafts shop in town where the craftwork is displayed on a daily basis for sale.

The following are examples of women who have been able to send their children to school from their meagre savings from the sale of the crafts:

- Teddy Anam, a widow, is a very hardworking and committed member who weaves beautiful baskets and makes necklaces and bracelets from paper beads. She has eight children under her care and she has supported them and paid their school fees. Her last-born, Helen, completed her Uganda Certificate of Education (UCE) last year, hoping to enter a tertiary institution if an opportunity comes her way. However, her mother is now facing challenges as she continues to help all of her children. Teddy joined Te-cwao in 2009 when she was unable to support the family after the death of her husband, who was killed by the Lord's Resistance Army rebels. I remember that she had no smile on her face when she came to Te-cwao for help. Now her life has changed and she thanks Te-cwao for the initiative that has uplifted her family. Despite her advanced age, she still weaves and moulds paper beads.
- Susan Amadi is a single mother with one son. He dropped out of school because Susan could not afford his school fees. Joining Te-

cwao in 2009 was a turning point in her life and that of her son, who has since returned to school. He is a brilliant boy performing well at Advanced Level of secondary education. Susan and her son are now living happily.

- James Ekwang, now 21 years old, survived. But both of his parents were killed during the insurgence. The same day his parents were killed, James dropped out of school. In 2010, his uncle introduced him to Te-cwao to be trained in craft making. James worked with commitment and dedication to make jewellery after the training. The money he earned allowed him to return to school. James worked during holidays to enable himself to raise fees for the subsequent terms in school as well as hospital bills. He completed his Comprehensive Nursing course in May 2015 from Good Samaritan School of Nursing in Lira. James still loves craftwork although he already has a profession in nursing. He states:"I am grateful to Te-cwao for making me who I am today."
- Teresa is a widow who lost her husband to HIV/AIDS. All her children dropped out of school, and they started selling pancakes on the streets just to survive. One day, Teresa came across a group of women weaving baskets and making paper beads at Te-cwao. She asked to join them because she had learned how to make baskets and beads in Mukono Town where her husband used to work. Since becoming a member, her children are now all back to school and she is able to support them.

The Piggery Project

Piggery is another of the income generating activities in which Te-cwao has invested. We started with six pigs in 2009, five females and one male with help from the government and the Northern Uganda Support Action Fund. To date we have been able to provide 106 piglets to 52 households. When the pigs deliver, a TYEA member is given a male and a female. The programme is sustainable and has always supported itself.

One example of a member who has benefited from the piggery project is Okello Benedict, a single father with five children. He was among the founding members of Te-cwao. Benedict received two piglets from Te-cwao in 2009 and now has 23 pigs, which he uses to support the family and pay for his children's education. He has also been able to construct a modern pig sty in his compound. One of his sons has completed vocational training in bricklaying and concrete practice from Adwoki Technical School.

Development Plans

As an association, Te-cwao hopes to step up our activities in the next project period by conducting trainings and evaluations. We are looking forward to conducting four leadership training sessions, each taking two days. The participants will be one from each category of people that we serve at TYEA; that is, one woman, one youth, one elderly person, one man, one widow and one representative of persons with disabilities. They will become our ambassadors in their respective villages, parishes and sub-counties. This activity will promote the empowerment of the communities and help people to improve their incomes after learning from the trainings. We hope to have at least two radio talk shows on the local stations as a way of creating awareness of the leadership trainings. The talk shows will reach approximately 500,000 people in the districts of Oyam, Kole, Lira, Apac, Dokolo, Amolatar, Alebtong, Otuke and other neighboring districts in the Acholi sub-region. We also hope to improve on the shows of our drama group, which focus on issues of social improvement. Broadcasting them on the local radio station is a way of combating poverty and domestic violence in the local population.

Another objective is to equip the community with a culture of saving and investing. Te-cwao has introduced a village savings and loan association (VSLA). Members can borrow to conduct personal business, paying back the loans at 10% interest. We will evaluate the goal by examining how much income is generated and saved through work with crafts, piglets and other activities. We will also begin taking part in local and district trade shows to increase the market potential for our products.

A new venture for TYEA will be plant cultivation. We intend to initiate a nursery tree centre as another income-generating activity extending in its outreach to areas beyond Lira. Te-cwao also hopes to begin a vegetable-growing programme to improve members' diets and their income from the sales. Vegetables selected will be short period crops that can be ready within three to six weeks.

Te-cwao plans to train all the members in bio-gas system construction to enhance the finances of members and the association itself. Earlier in TYEA's history, we were only able to help some members with this initiative. Our goal is to expand the programme and have biogas systems installed in all the homes of beneficiaries.

Finally, the association looks forward to informing the community about the importance of girl children's education, with hopes of eliminating the ideology of looking at the girl child as only a source of bride price. Through the education of girls and training of women, Te-cwao intends to empower women economically, which will reduce the rate of economic dependency on husbands even for very simple things such as salt, children's clothing. Sadly, such small purchases have been one cause of domestic violence. Regarding continuing education, Te-cwao hopes to improve on the reading culture of the community by lobbying for book aid from well-wishers who would like to improve the poor reading culture in homes.

Women's Cooperatives in Northern Uganda

As mentioned throughout our book, women continue to struggle for equal rights with men in northern Uganda. According to research conducted in 2013, 90% of rural Ugandan women work in agriculture, yet they receive less than 10% of extension services and credit, and they own only about 7% of the land (Coop Africa 2013). Such disproportionate help, of course, results in on-going poverty. Cooperativess that include agriculture, such as Te-cwao and its piggery project, are important for raising women's economic power and that of their children.

Cooperative organisations are one kind of community-based organisation (CBO). By nature, cooperative groups involve people who voluntarily join together to meet their needs in terms of economic, social and cultural needs. One sees this clearly upon coming up to Te-cwao's property. Men, women and children gather and engage in weaving, making beads and sewing. In 2011, I arrived to a joyful greeting of ululation and song. Mothers held their babies on their laps as they strung beads into necklaces and bracelets. I felt as though these young children were getting an early start in understanding a trade and the value of cooperative work.

Cooperatives hold values that help to empower women, such as equality, equal participation, education and caring for one another. They often include education not only about increasing skills and economics, but also about health. Some values include charity work for women who may be elderly or unable to work due to disabilities. They typically help new members engage in activities that boost their economic standing. Women who were previously isolated gain pride and self-esteem as they learn new skills, and this helps them to negotiate increased respect in their domestic lives. Studies show that involvement in women's cooperatives has not only improved conditions for women with respect to their husbands and other men, but also in the affairs of local politics and community affairs (CoopAfrica, 2013; Ferguson and Kepe, 2011). As the members learn from one another, they are able to increase their skills for leadership and strategising, giving them a larger presence and voice in their communities. Because local areas see the results of cooperative groups in terms of increased productivity and income, they are coming to realise that the model not only works to raise equality. Additionally, it makes good economic sense. Cooperatives that include savings and loans schemes also help the members become more financially savvy.

Women's cooperatives have certainly increased attention to women's rights, notice of women's capabilities, and social and financial health. Some cooperatives successfully move beyond a primary status of one group to a secondary status that involves representational meetings by women from several cooperatives. Banding together can result in even greater power for women. One successful example includes the Women's Advocacy Network, led by Grace Acan (Chapter Six).

These larger networks can also face challenges. Widening the networks sometimes leads to disputes between groups, as competition for economic gain can be considerable. Although local groups welcome funding from first-world countries, cross-cultural competence is essential to prevent a dark side of outside intervention from non-natives interfering with the decisions of local people. Westerners involved with aid in non-Western countries are often unable to see beyond their perspectives to recognise the strength of community sharing in many non-Western contexts. They can impose their competitive values onto those whom they finance, thus diminishing the power of the local women to form their own decisions.

Some women's cooperatives in Lira District are primarily engaged in creating non-agricultural products. These include baskets, jewellery and clothing. One of the problems for such organisations is that there are insufficient local markets for their products. Because they are small, they frequently do not have the knowledge, information, or finances to apply for "fair trade" status. Jody has made a small connection between both Te-cwao and Lecanto High School in Florida, which created a school club, "Ugandan Pearls" (or UP, as they like to refer to themselves, saying they are working to bring *up* the lives of Ugandan women and children). The students have raised several thousand dollars over three years by selling the women's products that Jody brings back from her travels. Still, Te-cwao could prosper much more with larger affiliations for the beautiful baskets, jewellery, women's purses and toys. Even so, these women and more like them continue to make progress.

As major international aid organisations and NGOs depart from northern Uganda to pursue more recent world crises, such as those in Syria, South Sudan and the Democratic Republic of the Congo, increasingly, the community-based organisations are seeking ways to become self-sustaining. Women such as Eunice and the other inspiring women in this book are leading the way.

6

A time for healing

Acan Grace

I want to help other women, those who came back from the bush, so they can move on with their lives and live a dignified life. ~ Acan Grace

I am truly sorry that my colleague Julia did not have the opportunity to meet Grace Acan during the time in which we conducted research for *Cold Water*. I first met Grace in August 2011, along with her family when her mother Consy invited me to dinner. I was honoured to meet a humble young woman with a remarkable story of escape from the LRA. In spite of the trauma of eight years of captivity with the rebels, Grace returned to school and completed her secondary education before continuing in Development Studies at Gulu University. When I met her again in 2013, she had completed her studies in Gulu and was a leader of the Women's Advocacy Network (WAN), a network of nine women's groups that are a part of the Justice and Reconciliation Project (JRP) in Gulu. Esther Atoo, Consy and I travelled to Gulu to deliver fifty goats to women in the groups so that they could gain an income by raising the livestock. What follows is Grace describing her escape, and her story of healing and hope after her return to her family and community.

* * *

My name is Acan Grace. I tell my story because I want the world to know that northern Uganda has suffered terribly. Many continue to struggle with life because they were abducted when they were young, so, on return, they cannot afford to go back to school or they have nowhere to work and no one to take care of their children with whom they have returned from captivity. And even after going to school, one can end up not getting employed for so many reasons like limited job opportunities, segregation at the work place, and so on. In the process of the LRA abductions, so many young girls were taken away. They were forcefully given to the rebels as wives and porters; and they came back with children who are now also suffering.

My mother, Ogwal Consy, has already related the story of my abduction in Chapter Three. The first day when we were abducted, we walked towards Sudan. Fourteen of us reached Sudan on 12th December 1996. The others remained in Uganda.

While in Uganda, sometimes we were beaten for reasons that we did not understand. Also the rebels would order us not to cry after the beatings. When we did cry, they would tell us to stop or else we would be beaten even more. So much suffering happened during those terrible eight years that I was held captive –hunger, thirst and attacks. We were forced to do farming for survival. Almost every year, together with other young girls, I had to learn how to cut grass for building huts.

My fellow captives were a source of strength. The rebels kept us apart, but whenever we could meet, we gave each other verbal support. They threatened to kill whoever would be found speaking to the other. It was difficult for us to talk to each other, but still the rebels could not prevent us from saying *hi*. When girls were brutally beaten, we would tell one another: "Please, keep up the struggle, move on," and "One day we will be free." In these small ways, we always encouraged each other. Even now, we feel we are family.

One afternoon, as about fifteen of us were walking to a place that I did not know, we accidentally came across gunmen who had laid an ambush in place. Unaware, we continued moving. The only thing that alerted us was gunshots at close range where I could even see the hands of one of the soldiers. I was the fourth in the line. The first three in front of me were shot. I survived by throwing away the baggage that was on my head and running for my dear life along an empty riverbed. Behind me I could hear the cries of two babies whose mothers were in front of me, which confirmed that their mothers were either captured or had been shot dead. I continued distancing myself away from the scene until I came to four other people who had also managed to survive the ambush, as the sound of gunshots continued. One of the men who had sustained an injury from the ambush did not want me to join the survivors, as he was afraid that my baby would make noise and reveal where we were. He later allowed me to join them and so I did, because he was the only person among us who knew the directions.

I walked blindly with the four without knowing where we were for at least two days before they made their first attempt to desert me in a place where I had no sense of direction. The attempt did not bear fruit: I sneaked after them, and they were surprised to see me again. But they kept on asking me to allow them to hide me somewhere in the bush where they would come back later to check on me. I refused as I did not trust them, and where they wanted to leave me was deep in the forest where I would end up either dying of hunger or being attacked by wild animals. However, after moving one whole night passing very close to two IDP camps, they tried again to abandon me in an area that I felt was not safe. They told me to stay behind as they scanned the security of the area. But they were planning to get rid of me, as they were afraid we would be captured if my baby cried.

So, that is how I managed to escape in the beginning. We followed a main road until we got to some thick bush where we hid. We had just some roasted beans to eat. There was no water, and I was very thirsty and cold, because I had thrown off my baggage in order to escape the ambush. My baby was completely naked. I had only that piece of clothing that I was tying her with on my back.

In the morning we started moving again, and reached a place where we saw signs that people were not very far away. We walked until late in the afternoon, when the other girls boiled beans and gave me some to me and my baby. After we had moved for about half an hour, they told me to wait while they went to pick some fresh beans for our next meal. That's when they left me. It was around two o'clock. I waited for them, but they did not come back. It became late. I realised I was alone. I went back to where they said they would get fresh beans, and I heard someone. But the grass was tall, so I could not see anybody, although I could hear someone was coming towards me, and we were going to collide. When the person realised someone was walking towards him, the person ran back. I also ran back very fast and hid somewhere. I thought there were soldiers who would capture me, so I hid and I waited until late in the evening. It was very dark when I went back to that *shamba* where I had been deserted. I collected some leaves and made a bed for myself. Then I slept. But I wondered: "How could these girls leave me and my child?" I was confused, and I did not know what to do. The rebels had told us that if the government soldiers caught us escaping, they would kill us. The rebels would also kill us if they caught us escaping. No side was safe, not even the civilians.

I spent my night there. The next day, I moved in search of food. I found a small hut that belonged to some people who had gone away to the fields. I was hungry, so I picked their saucepan and their maize flour, and I made some porridge for my child and myself. Then, I then left that place, and I continued with the hope of somehow making it home.

During the day, I had to keep moving, searching for an opportunity to get home in a safe way without meeting either the army or the civilians. I had to avoid the rebel groups, and I did not want to meet soldiers. I hoped that I could find a place where I could explain myself, but I was afraid of anyone else. After about a week, I was still trying to preserve a fire to keep us warm and to use for cooking.

Then it began to rain seriously, and the fire was put out. Now how was I going to survive?

The situation became too much for me. One morning, I walked out and said: "God, if this is the day you have prepared that I should die, then let me die today. If this is the day you have decided to let me stay alive, then this is my chance. I'm going." I just stood up and walked to the courtyard of the home near where I was hiding. The owners of the hut were also just returning from the IDP camp. We met, and I started trembling out of fear. I told them that I had been there for a week because my friends abandoned me and I had nowhere else to go.

The people then took me directly to the soldiers, who asked for so many things. I kept answering, "I don't know" or "I don't have anything." They asked what group I was moving with, but I avoided that question, because I feared they would return me to the bush to help them search for that rebel commander. So I said, "For me, it was a long time ago when I saw the rebels, so I was staying here all alone." The commander was the one in charge of the battalion whose ambush we entered when I made my escape. He kept telling me the names of those they killed in that ambush, so I realised it was my group that they had attacked. They transported me to another unit, and then handed me over to another commander, who took me to Gulu.

When I was brought to the barracks at Gulu, more authorities questioned me. I feared for my life. But someone told my father, who was on business in Gulu at the time, that I was being held by the military. He came to the location, where we were reunited.

I returned home in late September of 2004, eight years after my abduction, but I did not return to school until 2005. I could not go to the class that I wanted. I had to start again from Senior Two, as the syllabus had completely changed. Things were so different. I wanted to study. I also wanted to catch up with my friends. The other girls were already working; what else could I do other than study? All during those years in the bush, I thought about going to school. I said to myself: "Even if I am old, still I need to go back to school, when God helps me and I go back home." I realised I had to do this for my future.

I have studied development studies at Gulu University because I want to help women especially, because women are marginalised in my society. I also want to educate children. I care about human life. Life is so important. Children are important, and I really do not want to see a child suffering. If a child is crying, I want to know why. My first-born turned eight in 2011. I want to protect her and see that she gets a good education.

My parents have always supported me. They took care of my baby when I came back so I could finish school. Even during captivity, I can say that my friends always encouraged each other. That is why I want to help other women, those who came back from the bush, so they can move on with their lives and live a dignified life. I went to study at Gulu University because it was one of the two public universities where I was given a place, and secondly, I felt that it was a better option as I was offered the course that I had applied for.

I became involved with the Women's Advocacy Network because initially I was involved in a project that resulted in the formation of WAN. The initial project involved story-telling: a group of war-affected women shared their stories that led to the creation of their own personal history book based on their experiences during the war. However, during the story-telling sessions, many post-conflict issues such as stigmatisation, rejection of children born in captivity by either family members or the community, and other life challenges were expressed by the women. We, leaders of the project, felt that these issues could not just be ignored. So, the four of us came together and discussed how we could address the problems. The initial project, the Justice and Reconciliation Project (JRP), was not designed to manage the issues that evolved from the stories. We agreed that an advocacy platform should be created. It would involve all the groups in the story-telling project, because our analyses of the issues affecting women in the groups resulted in the same conclusions.

In a team of four, we decided on the name of the new forum, Women's Advocacy Network. We called a meeting for the nine groups by inviting 12 representatives, where we shared our new idea. An election of leaders took place in March 2011, and WAN kicked off in May. WAN started by creating awareness of what women were going through as a result of the war to stakeholders. Selected women organise and meet with those they think are a position to listen and act on their issues. With support from the JRP, WAN uses the media and music, dance and drama to explain the challenges. Afterwards, the women conduct community dialogues to inform and discuss with the local communities some of the issues, such as stigmatisation, land conflict and domestic violence, among others.

My work in WAN is to provide support in crucial areas where others cannot serve. For example, I attend meetings that are conducted in the local language and translate the proceedings in English, as most of those in the network are not in a position to read, write or speak English. I keep records of whatever happens and provide advice and ideas that are workable. In the future, I would like to see WAN become even more successful, as it swells my pride to see the lives of women, and in particular those who were affected during the war, changed socially, physically, economically and emotionally for the better.

Children in schools and expressive art therapy

Julia Byers and Jody McBrien

> Jane, a beautiful yet undersized girl in a Senior One class, was struggling with the stigma of being HIV positive. Looking for my eye contact and approval, Jane said that the group experience was one of the happiest times she had had all year. One of the most moving moments for me was when an older girl showed deep compassion for Jane by gently wrapping her arms around her, as Jane told her story through art.
> ~ Julia Byers

According to educators interviewed in Lira, approximately 50% of children are not in school, in spite of Uganda's adoption of both Universal Primary Education (UPE) and Universal Secondary Education (USE). There are many reasons for this; most are linked to poverty. Even though national schools are "free," parents must pay for uniforms, paper, writing implements, and books. As many are subsistence farmers, they cannot afford the little money these purchases require, especially if they have many children, which is typical of Ugandan families. There remains the challenge of girls' education, as it is still expected that educated boys, not girls, will be available to help their parents in their retirement (There is no national system for retirement or healthcare.). As mentioned earlier, many girls who attend primary school drop out when they reach puberty because of shared latrines where they are teased, advances by boy students and male teachers and early marriages arranged by parents. Children who do not attend school may not learn English, nor are they likely to learn occupational skills to move them out of extreme poverty. They are likely to "dig" for a living; most Ugandan households depend on subsistence farming (Tebusabwa n.d.). In 1980, 80% of females were engaged in agriculture but were twice as likely to be unpaid family workers as men (Kasirye 2011).

An additional dilemma exists for the fortunate few who are educated, as the Ugandan workplace is still not sufficiently advanced to need large numbers of highly educated residents. In a country where 60% of the population is under 24 years old, and nearly 50% are fourteen or younger (CIA 2103), it is troubling that 80% of those work-aged youth in northern Uganda are unemployed (Omona 2012). There are some who have spent tens of thousands of shillings to attend university or teacher training centres, only to end up with paltry salaries. The average teacher salary in the north is 200,000 to 300,000 Ugandan shillings ($78-117 US dollars, at the time of writing this chapter) per month, and sometimes they go two to three months without pay. This situation, of course, decreases morale and motivation. Students interviewed spoke of intoxicated teachers and teachers who simply do not show up for classes.

Our workshops have centred at three schools in Lira: Rachele, St Katherine and Barlonyo. Rachele Comprehensive School began as a rehabilitation centre for child soldiers and other abducted children returning from the war, and is named after Sister Rachele of St Mary's School in Aboke, a nun who heroically followed LRA rebels to demand the return of girls abducted from her school. Rehabilitation was critically needed to avoid psychopathic behaviours by formerly abducted children. However, prior to the opening of the centre, there were no efforts in the Lango sub-region to help. Between 2003 and 2006, the Centre helped 2,500 youth return from their lives in the bush, as either captured or rebel-born children, to community life.

The abuse the abducted children suffered was described as "one of the worst violations of children's rights anywhere in the world" (Ellison 2006, p. 11). In rehabilitation, many of the returned children exhibited symptoms of those who participated in a cult. They suffered from depression, a sense of meaninglessness, flashbacks, hallucinations, guilt and loneliness (Ellison 2006). Girls suffered the additional effects of stigma from bearing babies of terrorists and HIV infection. The objectives of the centre were to aid in the physical and psychological recovery of the children; aid in their reintegration to the community; help the community, itself traumatised, to forgive and reconcile with the children; and advocate the release of other children in captivity. Funded by the Belgian government, the centre was transformed into Rachele Comprehensive Secondary School in 2006 (comprehensive meaning that it would include vocational training as well as formal education). In 2007, the school transitioned to ownership by the Catholic Diocese of Lira. Belgium maintains a presence at the school in its Centre for Children in Vulnerable Situations, currently directed by Lieve Millisen.

St Katherine Secondary Education School for Girls is a government-funded boarding school serving approximately one thousand girls. Once one of the best girls' schools in Uganda, it continues to struggle after the LRA insurgency. During our July-August visit in 2013, teachers had not been paid in three months. Many were talking about returning to their villages to farm, as they would at least have food for sustenance. Girls interviewed there were remarkably articulate and engaged in their work. We noticed a marked difference between interviews there and at mixed gender schools. The girls had high hopes for skilled jobs, and they also had created projects to help themselves, such as starting clubs and internships to help them progress. They felt supported by one another regarding sexual issues in ways that girls from mixed gender schools did not. Still, many discussed their fears of being sent away due to problems such as paying school fees. Girls were discharged from the school if they could not pay their fees, and they had to stay away until they collected the required money. Many of these girls fear that lack of school fees will place them in the situation of early marriage and motherhood, thus jeopardising their opportunities to advance in the future.

Barlonyo Technical and Vocational Institute (BTVI) was built with Canadian funding and opened in 2010 with 85 students. A goal of the school was to insist that the community would not be defeated by the terrible massacre that occurred there in 2004, resulting in the brutal deaths of over 300 residents. By 2013 was educating over 200 students, and there were nearly 100 children in the Early Childhood Centre, created in 2012 to help young mothers enrolled BTVI. Over the past three years, the school has continued to develop self-sustainable activities: poultry, pigs, tilapia, bees, oxen to plough fields, and more.

Capturing invisible time

As international outsiders, we wanted to capture our collective time in Uganda with some sense of meaning. Jody attempted to make a time schedule. We changed it. Changes in our colleagues' schedules surfaced again and again. Our notion of facilitating groups and conducting research interviews clearly began as a Western desire to organise in some fashion. However, our mutual desires to make meetings work created close bonds, and we succeeded in arriving at meeting times that were filled with meaning. Our colleagues appeared surprised when we reminded them that we had to leave. We all wanted more time.

After our initial arrival in Uganda, it took over eight hours to travel from Entebbe to Lira with our hosts who made stops in Kampala to get car parts fixed. Trying to leave Kampala, we wove through the human and car traffic of a city exposed to the bare necessities of life. We travelled through the poorer districts of the city witnessing a tapestry of humanity trying to make ends meet by selling any wares they could. Limp chickens with their feathers still on bounced off bicycle handles as the owners cycled by under the sweltering sun. Swells of vegetables displayed in rows lined the streets with the vendors crouched on the ground for hours in the hope of sales. As a white outsider, I felt conflicted about whether or not I should smile at passers-by or remain seemingly disconnected, even though my whiteness felt like porcelain that could easily break. Finally leaving the city, we travelled through remote villages composed of grass huts and local red clay. Curious children clad in T-shirts and baggy shorts sat at the edge of the road seemingly searching for something to happen. With the increasing discomfort of our car seat that had little support and no legroom, Jody and I clutched our backpacks on our laps in anticipation of finally arriving in Lira.

In the small villages, there is often no electricity, yet our modest hotel did have intermittent power. After arriving at Lira Hotel, I discovered rips in my mosquito netting and cracks in my hotel door, exposing holes to invite one of the world's most powerful miniature hunters – the mosquito – onto my sensitive body. People in the town would gather at the Lira Hotel to view soccer games on the TV, or come to a dance that started at 10 or 11pm and finished at about 4 am. Other competing 24/7 "discos" would play further into the early morning.

The local town, largely comprised of buildings made from local clay brick and cement, was animated with bicycles and *boda boda*s (a local variety of taxi in which transportation is on a motorcycle or bicycle). Very few cars were on the roads. People mainly walked or rode their bicycles on the British side of traffic. Every few feet another Ugandan woman sat beside her wares or food from her garden to be sold. Loosely hung American shoes blew in the wind to beckon passers-by. Local stalls of vegetables, fruits, meat, clothing, shoes, school supplies, backpacks and other necessities made a tapestry of coloured threads into a visual cacophony. Just outside the town proper, Te-cwao offered its handmade articles of paper beads, baskets and stuffed animals to potential purchasers.

St Katherine Secondary School for Girls

We drove to St Katherine Secondary School for Girls at the edge of the main road. Depending on their level of confidence or comfort, car drivers sped by the unassuming flow of children and adults on both sides of the narrow streets. Emma, a teacher and counsellor at St Katherine, drove us carefully through the intermittent cows, sheep and goats joining the pedestrians along the roadways. Turning off the main drag, her car that had the driver's door permanently locked from the outside bumped and gyrated along the red clay dust and loose stones on the ground to get to the campus. In the yard, wooden placards dotted the grounds of a central old British colonial style building, reminding students and staff to be friends with HIV positive people, keep hope and be well.

As was the local custom, we first sat in the headmistress's office, eager to begin our time with the adolescent girls. Emma had identified 12 girls who were either abductees, HIV carriers, orphans, or severely deprived young women who would benefit from our psychosocial group experiences. Emma was trained as a counselling psychologist from the Uganda Christian University Mukono. She generously gave us her time and offered to follow up with any of the girls who needed additional help after we had left. Emma and two other female teachers provided Jody and me with a sense of camaraderie during our time at the school. They also gave practical assistance in translating English into Leblango, although the teachers were reluctant to let the girls speak their native language in the dormitories and at school. Our challenge was to provide the girls with new community building activities in which to gain a sense of safety, trust and companionship, hopefully re-engaging with a positive sense of self and others.

Under a shaded tree within the school property, the dutiful girls brought chairs for the teachers while the students sat on the ground. Changing the dynamic, I encouraged all the girls to have chairs or suggested that all of us sit on the grass. This seemed to raise everyone's eyebrows in seemingly a defiant act from their normal routine. In a welcoming gesture, Jody and I began by singing a welcome song. For every song Jody and I taught the girls, we encouraged them to teach us a song of welcome or good-bye. We provided several dancing and singing activities so the girls could laugh, giggle and join together to create a sense of safety and community within our small group.

To make a bridge between the contexts of the environment, we asked the girls to create a drawing representing their name and a "fantasy name" to help us get to know them. This provided a sense of security in the task and added an expectation of sharing surprises. Most girls provided their Ugandan name and the Christian name given to them.

The goal of the psychosocial intervention was to aid in the continuum of building resilience and strength, especially to those who had terrible loss as a result of the civil uprising of Kony and the LRA. The devastation of Kony's abuse left a trail of destruction, pain and deep levels of grief. Many of the girls had scarred slash marks on their arms and legs, inflicted from being captured or disobedient during the abductions. As Susan Gere and I wrote in "Time and Temporality" (2007), a psychologically controversial issue is whether to seal over the trauma or allow people to tell their narrative stories supported by the group community. As outsiders, we knew our role represented professional women who modelled the promise of full career lives, motherhood and travel beyond the African continent. Our presence meant that life beyond Lira could be possibly tempered by luck, fortune, or sheer blatant hope for support beyond what most families could manage. Most girls knew the privilege of even being allowed to go to school was often beyond families' financial capacities.

Within this context, of not opening too much nor closing down those who needed emotional support for their current lives or troubling memories, we asked the girls to find three objects in the yard, school, or dormitory that represented their past, present and future. We then gave the girls options to use watercolour paint, oil pastels, or coloured pencils to copy, outline, or symbolically illustrate their chosen items. For many girls, the use of watercolour paints and brushes was a new experience that they seemed to relish. The girls appeared gleeful with the radiant colours of the supplies that we had carried in our overloaded suitcases. We hoped they could continue to enjoy the art supplies after we had returned to the US. We gathered the girls into three small groups so that a teacher could translate and be more intimately engaged with the girls.

The teachers gathered information about the meaning or the function of each object. Many girls chose to express the functional use of getting fruit or making clothes to be sold to take care of their family members. Due to our time limitation and the girls' hunger (dinner was served between 5:30 - 6:00 pm, and we could only work with them after their classes were over), we chose to focus on one child in each group to follow up with over our subsequent gatherings to monitor their progress in the group experience. In the older group, we focused on Jane, a beautiful yet undersized girl in a Senior One class, who was struggling with the stigma of being HIV positive. She feared rejection by most people and was struggling to feel she had a future since being labelled as "one of those girls" by the community. Looking for my eye contact and approval, Jane told one teacher that the group experience was one of the happiest times she had had all year. One of the most dramatic and moving moments for me was when an older girl showed deep compassion for Jane by gently wrapping her arms around her, as Jane told her story through art. Her raised self-esteem in this moment was clearly visible in her soulful eyes.

Tracy had come from a small village and was grieving the death of her mother from HIV. Kony's army had killed one of her brothers, and her father had abandoned the family. Not only was she deeply saddened by her mother's death and her sense of being an orphan, she also feared the lack of ability to remain in school since her aunt and extended family were not sure if they could continue to support her school fees. With fear and longing in her eyes, Tracy asked for the group to honour the dignity of her mother. Tracy was one of the abducted girls who was forced into the bush as a sex slave and returned to the suffering of villagers rejecting her.

Much to our surprise, Tracy exhibited an eagerness to be spontaneous with paint. She became childlike in her random exploration of the outline of the natural stone and twig that she had gathered. She clearly expressed a cathartic release of energy with her art and let out a big sigh with her peers. Choosing natural objects to express herself revealed how she had coped in the gruesome hours of being trapped in the bush with the army.

Our gatherings were delayed in the next few days due to a school assembly. This school event, which was supposed to start in the morning, began in the afternoon, and finished just before supper. Again, Jody and I experienced the invisible time barrier that conflicted with our Western expectations of a schedule. We were informed of the unplanned change while we were actually driving again to the site, burdened with carrying our art supplies in awkward, heavy bags. Our plan needed to be modified. Countless girls' emotional loads of scarred life experiences beyond our imagination dwarfed the physical weight we carried. Unfortunately, we needed to speed up our time with the girls, knowing that we were still committed to visiting other school sites. Additionally, the unforeseen circumstances of Jody becoming ill with a respiratory infection as a result of travelling along the dusty red clay roads modified our collective time. We also learned that Eunice, the Director of Te-cwao, whom we had both hugged only two days before, had contracted malaria and typhoid fever. The potential for contracting the diseases ourselves was not an abstract concept. We went to see Eunice a second time, as Jody had brought some money collected by the high school students in Lecanto, Florida, who sold Te-cwao's handicrafts. We hoped that the funds would help her get medical treatment. With the geographic distance of the other schools, we were forced to delay our time at St Katherine School until the next week.

When we were scheduled to return to St Katherine, Jody was too sick to attend the session, so I planned a more condensed, creative time with the girls to offer opportunities to seal over or express their narratives of trauma. Using metaphoric language, behaviours and characters found in stories about African animals, I invited the girls to make miniature clay animals to express their group experience. After our introductory singing and dancing together, we huddled in a circle, crouching on the ground with our fingers moulding clay and animating the creatures in creative play. I had brought some handmade miniature animals – a giraffe, a turtle, dog, and cat – and shared them in our intimate circle. The girls laughed and enjoyed each other as we spontaneously played, passing the animals between us and animating their characters. Then, I placed a ball of sculpting clay into each of the girls' hands so that they could make their own animals that they liked or disliked. We then broke out into three small groups to create collective stories about the clay animals, beginning with "Once upon a time…"

Suddenly the clouds in the sky erupted into a downpour of rain. This forced us to find shelter indoors because the tree could not hold all the raindrops to protect us. We quickly ran to a schoolhouse building that had fallen into disrepair, yet still had enough space for us to huddle together and exchange our stories. Perhaps the intimacy of being together in a cramped space added to the flavour of the narratives told. The following tales were told from the three different groups.

***

Once upon a time, there was a turtle and a bird. The turtle told the bird that he wanted to fly. The bird glued wings onto the Turtle. As he started to fly, the glue started melting. He soon fell onto the stones below and cracked his back. That is why turtles now have cracks on their backs.

***

Two friends, called Rabbit and Hyena, were neighbours. Hyena invited Rabbit to go visit Leopard to give him a gift. On the way, he met Elephant and other animal friends.

Hyena told Rabbit to greet others and to follow them like hunters follow dogs.

Making fun of the animals, the Hyena put down his gift basket containing baby rabbits to go light a cigarette. Nearby, Rabbit was left to take charge of the covered basket.

To his surprise, he peaked into the basket finding out that the babies were his own babies. Rabbit decided to run back home and put baby hyenas in the basket instead.

Hyena continued travelling with the gift basket, not knowing what was inside. Hyena then met more groups of friends and told them to follow him. Rabbit replied, "Wisdom does not belong to only one man." When they all reached the family of the leopards, Hyena instructed everyone that a meal was going to be made to celebrate their coming together. All were invited to dinner; mother leopard cooked the contents of the basket. Rabbit said, that the room was too hot to stay inside and said he would eat his dinner outside. While Hyena was eating, Rabbit said, "Eat one piece,

Crush it well; you may crush your own flesh. Wisdom is stronger than strength!"

***

There once lived a giraffe and a leopard. One day, as they were walking along a road, they stopped to have a meeting with other animals. They talked about killing the giraffe because he had too nice a colour in the kingdom. When giraffe got word that the animals wanted to kill him, he ran away.

As he was running, other animals saw him from a distance. He tried to hide behind a certain tree but he couldn't see where the other animals were. He had to scratch his neck so the other animals knew where he was, since the tree didn't cover him up. Then, he started eating food from other animal gardens without permission. When he was eating the other animals sneaked up and killed him. All the other animals were happy that he was finally dead.

* * *

Emma and I gently reframed the metaphoric stories acknowledging the complex feelings that everyone has when they are treated unfairly, betrayed, or worse. We talked about the resilient creativity of the girls combined with the strength of the community of women to give each other hope and empathy. We told them that their aggressive thoughts were a normal phase of trauma recovery. We encouraged the girls to honour each other in the small groups in their new and old friendships. Most girls reviewed the group time together and provided words such as *happy*, *content*, and *peaceful* after the gatherings, eager to please the facilitators. One girl, Tracy, had the courage to express her feelings that the workshops were interesting, but she was still clearly holding the sadness of her mother's recent death. In response, we honoured her mother again by providing our gestural good-byes. We broadened her feelings to honour the legacy of other significant others who had died. Finding the attention and unity within the group, Tracy seemed to relax and feel comforted by the community support. We counselled the girls to pass what they had learned forward in honouring their own achievements for the pride of the people and families that loved them. While we listened with our eyes and our hearts, we were aware of the ever present need for more time.

Rachele Comprehensive School

The next secondary school, Rachele Comprehensive School, appeared to be a more highly funded school with obvious improvements in building structures. It even had a new large library, although there were no books on the wall-to-wall shelves. The hope for purchasing or having donated books was clearly evident. Many students were using the empty library space to work on their homework.

Upon our arrival, we met with the principal of the school who introduced us to two Belgian counselling interns from the University of Belgium. For six months, these ambitious young women hoped to make a difference at the Belgian-financed and -operated centre called the Centre for Children in Vulnerable Situations, located on the school campus. We asked the interns to join us in the psychosocial group of girls so they could follow up with any girls who appeared to need continuing counselling after we had left. The interns had had difficulty in gaining access to the students' trust as students were not used to seeking help or discussing vulnerable issues to a stranger. The administrators of the school had invited the interns to accompany them on HIV training to the villages and other health related topics, but everyone spoke Leblango and frequently did not provide enough translation.

The principal had gathered male and female students together for our visit, not quite understanding or believing that for this initiative, we only wanted to work with young women. Since they had gathered a large group of students, the principal wanted us to interview the male child soldiers who were returned to Lira and were making progress in the secondary levels of schools. The principal chose the head boy and two other sixteen-year olds who had expressed they were coming to terms with their past and wanted to share their ambitions for the future. It felt inappropriate not to honour the school's request and the young men's pride at being chosen to speak about their chance to renew their lives. As Jody and I listened to the resilient experiences and struggles they had endured, I could not help but think what these children had done under Kony's rule and the existential crisis of being at the wrong place at the wrong time. Yet now, they expressed feeling in the right time and place to move on with their lives to support their families. Their main motivation depended on their ability to provide for their families.

With this emotionally felt backdrop, we continued to facilitate the same psychosocial support basic protocol in welcoming the newly selected twelve girls from different classes. These girls were chosen with similar backgrounds of abduction, rape, being orphaned, or living with HIV. We wanted to encourage and witness their resilience and coping skills; support their hopes; and empower their voices as women. Together with the interns, we formed three small groups to encourage the girls to find objects that represented past, present and future time. Perhaps, the most significant outcome was that some of the girls now felt comfortable enough to approach the interns for psychological and emotional support. The interns had been looking for ways to be invited in the community in which the language had been a real barrier. Through the openness of the arts, the girls knew that there was an accepting space to share their personal challenges. They appeared more open to engage. We consciously left art supplies for the counsellors to continue facilitating the expressive groups. We knew that a psychiatrist would be coming to the school one month later. Our role, if you will, was to warm up the community to supportive interventions through the arts.

Barlonyo Technical and Vocational Institute

Twenty-six kilometres from Lira, down a dirt road with acres of sunflowers planted as crops for cooking oil along each side of the road, Jody and I rode with Esther Atoo and her husband, Solomon Adiyo, to arrive at BTVI. Beside the school lies a mass memorial gravesite dedicated to 301 people killed by the Lord's Resistance Army in February 2004. The solid concrete graves lie in a horseshoe shaped structure that forms a community of murdered loved ones. Dirt and concrete seal over their stories of when they were forced into their huts and burned alive, with those attempting to escape cut down by rebels with machetes. The Ugandan government recorded on the monument plaque that 121 had died in the Barlonyo massacre, but survivors we met explained that the death toll reached 301.

On February 21, 2004, the LRA entered the Barlonyo IDP camp and started shooting. They forced families into their grass-thatched homes, which they ignited, killing the inhabitants. Adults and children who fled into the surrounding bush were pursued by rebels who caught and killed them on the spot. A fortunate few were able to escape and save their lives (JRP 2009). The devastating actions of Kony's rebels left the Barlonyo community in shock and despair. Ultimately, however, they chose not to follow a path of despair, but of resistance and hope. BTVI is a symbol of their determination to succeed.

The school, directed by Solomon, focused on rehabilitating war-affected youth by providing trainable vocational skills in agriculture, bricklaying, and tailoring. When we visited, the school had one female and two male dormitories, with about 150 students living in cramped, but neat quarters. There were three roofed classrooms, with open spaces in walls instead of windows. One structure made from local clay bricks and cement was outlined, but no floors or ceilings were installed yet. While waiting for the funds to complete the project, the school had built a huge slate blackboard affixed to the wall, in anticipation of additional students. Several feet from the main building, the school had built two ponds to farm tilapia to be eaten or sold. As there was no running water in the town or at the school, water was brought to pour into two main caldrons in the centre of the school grounds to use for cooking, cleaning and drinking after purification. As outsiders, Jody and I were constantly very aware of the cold bottled waters that we cradled in our hands.

The main office was near a classroom building. It consisted of two small rooms where staff gathered or, in our case, where the visitors were welcomed. Solomon and his teachers prepared a table with a white lace tablecloth and three table top flags ceremoniously waiting for our arrival. The Ugandan, American and Canadian flags stood as reminders of our respective homes and the diplomacy in honouring the backbone of our collective societies. Later, the same heavy wooden table was moved and placed under the central tree on the outer property when all the students and staff assembled to greet us, their guests.

When we arrived at BTVI in 2012, the whole community warmly welcomed us. As we drove up the circular dirt pathway to the central office, teachers and students looked eager as the foreign Wazungu (White people) arrived. After being introduced to the principal and teachers, Solomon Adiyo, the school's director, instructed the community to gather under the shade of the large tree.

All the students carried metal and wooden chairs under the tree and waited until a group of student musicians gathered. One by one, the Principal, Vice Principal, Head Teacher and Head Student addressed the assembly, welcoming their guests. Then the drama and musical performances began with a flurry of activity. After all the youth had sung the national anthem of Uganda, students played traditional handmade instruments of the olengter (similar to the zylophone), bull (drum), ajaya (shakers), okeme (local guitar), and the gwata (a bowl with multiple uses and sounds) – having rehearsed for many hours. With enthusiasm, the proud youth sang boldly and animatedly. Subsequently, a small group of boys and girls re-enacted a dramatic play and dance. The dance mirrored the goal of the school, not to be defeated by the brutality of the massacre that took place there. About ten girls put on brightly coloured grass skirts over their school uniforms to perform an original native dance of their region. The young men also participated with a dramatic performance of rising above slavery. With passionate voices and strong bodies, they danced in a circle kicking up dust from the ground as if their feet were on fire. Jody and I sat in awe as we were honoured by this community that welcomed us with enthusiastic and inquisitive smiles.

In accordance, for the ceremony, Jody and I each spoke respectively, reminding them of our purpose and goal in returning and honouring their lives since Jody's last visit. In less than a year, the school had made an additional building structure for a piggery project with half a dozen pigs, two new latrines (separated for boys and girls), and a strong shelter for the kitchen (which was previously outside, consisting of only a wood fire with a pot hanging above it). The regular lunch meal of porridge and evening meal of beans actively boiled in a huge metal pot in the new kitchen, fuelled by the fire of local dried wood and ashes. No electricity or power was evident in any of the buildings.

After all the introductions, welcome songs and goodwill wishes were expressed, the teachers chose twelve girls to accompany us to a space where we could work together. As was the case at St Katherine's School for Girls, we felt uncomfortable "choosing" girls to participate in the group, since all wanted to attend the sessions. Choosing felt like an uncomfortable affair, especially considering how Kony had made a show of choosing people to live and die in this same area years ago. Our art supplies, however, were limited, so, decisions had to be made on who could participate. We devised activities that girls would teach to the broader community and ended our time together back in the whole group. The task of identifying only girls to work with raised several eyebrows since boys or young men were frequently selected as school representatives. As previously discussed, girls in Uganda are often considered secondary citizens and they are unaccustomed to attention. However, Barlonyo is working towards gender equality in the school setting.

When Jody went back a year later for a follow-up art workshop, all of the available girls (about 30 that day) were brought into a classroom with sewing machines on all the tables so that all of them could participate. Quarters were cramped, but all of the girls happily shared the markers and crayons amongst themselves and held up their drawings with pride. The school had grown greatly over the year since we first visited, with the new Barlonyo Early Childhood Development Centre (a nursery school) opened on the BTVI campus. It allowed for local preschool youth and those of young mothers attending Barlonyo to remain in classes while their children were educated in the nursery school and tended to in the day-care facilities. This was a step forward in helping young women to succeed.

With the outside heat of 32 degrees (90 degrees Fahrenheit), at first, we chose to meet under the central tree. A few days later, when we returned to the school, we redesigned our time to spend the entire day with the girls due to the long distance and hours it took us to travel there. During our second visit, we wanted more privacy than under the central tree as the male students working outside learning how to build structures looked on curiously. At first, the teachers instructed a male class to leave their classroom space so we could work in a shaded area, but we did not want to disturb their classes. Searching for alternative space, we found that one-third of the girls' dormitory room was a cement open space. We created our intimate space in the dormitory, where no one would be re-located and the girls would have privacy.

In order to make this happen, girls quickly began mopping the floor with rags making our space void of dirt, so we all could take our shoes off and make a seated circle on the floor. Other girls swept the perimeter of the space with brooms made from the brush in the area, noticeably bending over to touch the ground. Jody gently suggested that in America we add a long stick to the brush to avoid bending over while sweeping. The girls just shrugged and carried on as if to say, how is that going to help us now? At that moment, I realised just how remote we were in the bush. I acutely felt our whiteness and our privilege. When the girls felt they had cleaned the area sufficiently, we began.

We began by singing and dancing before asking the girls to do the similar task that had been successful in the other Lira schools. Again, we asked the girls to find objects that represented their past, present and future, and to create an image with all three elements as a way to encourage and validate their skills. Some girls appeared delighted with the soothing quality of using new paintbrushes and exploring different ways of expressing their lives. Others seemed a little wary and sat by each other with a tendency to copy each other. We had established that every girl would have a "buddy" with whom to both talk and play art together. This appeared even more valuable with this group of young women who lacked the social interactions, confidence and skills of those in the bigger town life of Lira. Barlonyo is a small rural village miles from the town of Lira. This school was more vocational in its orientation and the students were more directly affected by the horrors of Kony's army.

As the artwork evolved, we better understood who these girls were. They were most directly and traumatically struck by the war. Survivors and observers of the Barlonyo massacre, the girls' memories were vivid as they drew their homes on fire, family members dismembered by the machetes of the soldiers, coffins and even more horrific events experienced by family members who were forced to kill family members or be killed themselves. For others, many paintings contained army guns, expressing that they had witnessed or had felt the power of the weapon themselves.

The task of creating images of the present appeared therapeutic as the girls talked and explained how the school had provided them with food, shelter and new hopes of acquiring marketable skills. The level of detail in a drawing of a sewing machine or the pattern of a dress or eating together at a table provided evidence of binding their anxiety as well as re-tooling their thoughts into more positive and hopeful areas of new life. The girls spoke with full optimism of gaining and mastering skills. Many drew their future depicting the success of their learned skills to provide for their families. Some used the metaphors of flowers and plants blossoming as they hoped to bear children and live full lives one day. In comparison to the other girls' groups in previous schools, these girls silently walked to their teacher with their paintings, allowing her to tell their stories for them. As the teacher spoke, the girls' eyes searched for validation.

Their faces and their bodies showed truths that no child should ever witness. Many tortured marks were left behind on their black skin. The keloid nature of their skin tends to bubble and rise when a slash or burn disrupts the texture. Sometimes, it was hard to look at their eyes when I wanted to stare at the scars and ask more questions. Intuitively, it was not the place or time to open up the symbolic wounds, unless the girl opened them voluntarily. This reinforced the respect of knowing when to open or seal over real and psychological wounds without knowing if we would ever return.

Daniel Siegel, author of *Mindsight* (2010), and many other psycho-neurologic professionals concur that creating physical activities to literally re-wire the brain or replace intrusive thoughts or memories can be acquired through physical sensory activities. I had a sense that we needed art supplies that could represent psychological attachment metaphors for the young women to re-engage with their peers. Bringing highly coloured thick embroidery thread, which was both light in weight and small to pack in the suitcases, served to be helpful. As I wrote in a 2010 journal article (Byers, 2010), the medium of string, wire, thread, wool, and so on can serve as a way to explore and re-engage with understanding how traumatised populations can literally rewire themselves, making metaphoric and real connections to improve interpersonal skills along with a sense of bonding together.

In preparation for the activity, Jody and I had practised how to make and how to teach the making of "Friendship Bracelets." Many cultures have an intuitive inter-generational way of weaving, and we wanted to invite different methods of attaching or weaving threads together. We reinforced the importance that the activity was created between two people taking turns leading, aiding, and creating the process. Both of us had ideas about what different weaves could look like and we began to practise our joint interconnection. An interested hostess in one of the hotels we stayed at in Entebbe looked on curiously as we wove together on Jody's skirt as a foundation.

The native woman started chatting with us about how she wanted different ideas of crafts to share with her pre-adolescent daughter. She spoke about how it was getting harder to connect with her child. The final mastery of our woven bracelet was truly impressive to her, and we offered it to her as a gift for her daughter. Back in Barlonyo, Jody perfected the skill of weaving threads through using our fingers as the warp and weft of crafted fabric. Using separate fingers to keep the threads organised and one of the paintbrushes as an anchor created a rhythmic flow.

As the room filled with pairs of students eagerly grabbing for the multi-coloured threads, each team found its own ways of creating the bracelets. Two groups in particular were able to rhythmically establish a dance of sorts, keeping the movements smooth and the tension of the string taunt. Others appeared mismatched in their attempts, trying to find ways of being in harmony with each other. All methods were encouraged. Our fall-back was the weave that Jody and I mastered, creating a colourful twirling design. Similar to "Eye Movement Desensitisation and Reprocessing" (EMDR), a physical therapeutic response for traumatised people to re-condition their emotional states and self-regulate, the physical back and forth motion of the bracelet weaving seemed to replace the emotional tension that had been projected in the war images many girls had experienced and expressed in their drawings and paintings. The girls appeared focused towards building a sense of mastery and connectedness. We also encouraged this "special" group of twelve girls to spend additional time instructing the other girls who were unable to be part of the group so they could make something new together.

We left the art supplies and encouraged the girls to think about other uses of making and/or potentially selling their creative work. We summarised and honoured the shared experiences of the day and gathered again under the large tree with all the girls from the school to sing and dance together. We ended by tossing a large ball of multi-coloured yarn from girl to girl, having each girl hold the yarn before tossing the ball. This created a web of colour connecting all of the girls. The girls laughed joyfully when we brought out containers of bubbles for them to blow, as they had never done this before, and they laughed as they made and chased soap bubbles in the air. We thanked them for their continuing community development in the sisterhood of life and told the teachers how grateful we were to have their name drawings collected from the whole community.

Later that night, Jody and I met again with Emma and reviewed the preparations for the 2012 International Woman's Day celebrations. The synopsis for Uganda included the goal that Ugandan girls would need to walk no more than one and a half kilometres to collect water for their families (International Women's Day 2012). This goal reiterates a 2005 goal of the Ugandan government that "65% of the population in Uganda are within one and a half kilometres of safe water by the year 2005" (WELL 2003). From our conversations and experiences, many girls have to walk many miles every day to carry water for their families. In the remote village of Barlonyo and the new vocational school, the goal demonstrated its importance. The water that girls used to mop the cement floor was the same water we dipped the paintbrushes into and saved to wash our feet, taking off the grit of the local dirt. As for drinking, we went back to our now warm bottled water in the cramped teachers' room and waited for Solomon, the director of the school, to generously drive us back to our hotel. There was no other way to get back to town than the forty-five-minute car ride, other than walking for several hours on the dirt road in the tropical heat.

One of the compassionate fatigue symptoms of international crisis intervention work is the feeling of guilt associated to being one of the lucky few in the world who have opportunities for this kind of travel due to our far greater financial resources. As I write this chapter, a few short weeks after returning to the US, I still feel the challenges of re-integrating into a contemporary first world society that takes for granted simple luxuries of running water for drinking, cleaning and toiletries. I also remember the water in some Ugandan girls' eyes as they reached out for help. Buddhists say, "Anyone, at any time, can be your teacher if you are open to learning." Although I embarked on my Ugandan journey with the thought of being a teacher, I could not help but realise how much more I had been a student of these young girls.

8

Lives in pictures

Julia Byers and Jody McBrien

Girls of Rachele Secondary School, Barlonyo Technical and Vocational Institute (BTVI), and St Katherine Senior Secondary School

"The aim of art is to represent not the outward appearance of things, but their inward significance." ~Aristotle

The following "living artworks" were created during trips to Lira, Uganda in 2012 and 2013. These photos and artworks serve to document the portraiture of our experiences with the women in Lira. All of the images portray living with or surviving post-war traumas and "moving forward," as Emma repeatedly told us in our last trip in July, 2013. "How are you?" we asked her. "Moving," was always her response.

The adage "a picture tells a thousand words" is especially poignant when trauma experienced by the artists prevents them from discussing their histories verbally. Memories too horrible to speak in words are often expressed in art, whether it be paint, pencil, music, dance, or drama. As an art therapist, I was continually sensitive to a "trauma-informed approach" (Byers and Alfonso 2012; Malchiodi 2012), focusing on the resilience and strengths of individuals within the community. The graphic depictions of traumatic experiences were still very real for the abducted and injured girls. As outsiders, we witnessed a routine of the schools encouraging their students to tell their stories. Former UN workers and NGOs such as the Unity Project with psychiatrist Dr John Woodall, and others, had visited the girls; and the staff wanted the girls to get recognition and validation for telling their stories. With the small group of participants in the brief humanitarian art relief intervention, it felt like their past was still present in the room.

Art works by children at Rachele, Barlonyo, and St Katherine schools over the past three years indicate a kaleidoscope of tragedy and hope. Girls have drawn detailed pictures of murder, huts on fire and coffins, signifying their war years as well as sewing machines, flowers and occupations that point to their future hopes. The paintings tend to use present experiences to represent the solidarity of the community schools as hope for the future. Most of the future aspirations were depicted with the desire to have families or vocational work. The interactional expressive play or arts in music, words, dance and 3-D art work, are not necessarily shown in the photos, but are discussed in the other chapters. As a sense of artifacts within qualitative arts-based inquiry, these selected images are shown to be witnessed by others rather than analysed or interpreted.

Over the past three years, we have collected nearly 100 drawing and paintings by girls at the three schools where we have presented workshops. We have chosen to share 11 here that represent the themes and preoccupations of the girls with whom we have worked.

Lives in pictures

Photo of presenters at ICSD 2013: *(Left to right)* Jody McBrien, Okite Emma, Kia Betty, Atoo Esther, Julia Byers

Photo of presenters and USF student Ashley: *(Left to right)* Julia Byers, Okite Emma, Ashley Metelus, Jody McBrien, Kia Betty, and Atoo Esther

Rachele School in Lira: Expressive arts-based workshop, July 2013

Julia and girls at Rachele: Rachele School, Lira, Uganda: Expressive arts-based workshop using recycled CDs for community building interactive communication. The discs were initially created as name tags representing the person's identity and images or words depicting what was most important in their lives, followed by playing with the discs as spinners or toppers to experience spontaneous movement and play within the small group community intervention, and finally collectively stringing the discs together demonstrating group connectivity.

Lives in pictures 107

Burning Houses, Barlonyo Technical and Vocational School (BTVI), 2012: The past was depicted as the violence associated with Kony's army who purposefully ignited the local homes and tribal communities. The present is illustrated by the attention to detail in the local natural environment and the branches of the people that are important to this girl's life. The house in the lower right is her dream of having a family and a safe home in the future.

Child Soldier, BTVI, 2012: This image depicts a girl's experience of being forced to be a child soldier in Kony's army and the telling of the horrendous stories of Kony's violence within the communities. The present is represented by the tree under which the community now gathers for music, songs and sharing of stories that reunite the local culture. The house on the right is, again, hopes for the future in attaining a safe, strong structure of a dwelling.

Dreams, BTVI, 2012: The detail in which the sewing machine is depicted represents the present focus of this girl's life creating meaning for her new role and life in society as a tailor when she graduates. The burning house strongly depicts the loss of family and materials due to the violence of Kony's army. The pattern of dresses and shirts on the right provides a structure for the hope of who she will become as a mother and provider.

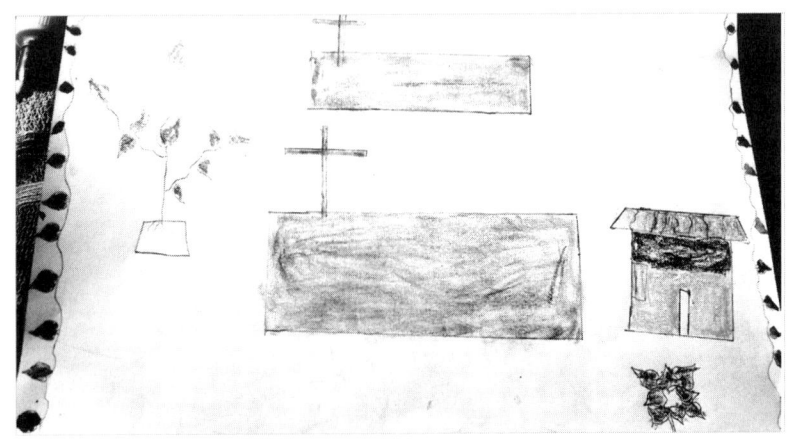

Family Graves, BTVI, 2012: Within yards of the of the BTVI rest the Barlonyo Memorial Graves. This girl was careful to mention that she had been orphaned by the murders of her parents who currently rest within the memorial site. Close by, she now waters a cassava plant (on the left of the page) whose roots are a staple food for local Ugandans. On the right is another depiction of her hope for her own home.

Lives in pictures

Kony's Guns, BTVI, 2012: Strongest in this image is a heart to symbolise all the people in this girl's life who were important to her. The military gun, central to this painting, still remains prominent in her life. New growth is evident in her dream of wanting a sense of family, as depicted in the local flora in the top left corner.

Memory, BTVI, 2012: This girl witnessed the killing of family members and the injuries sustained by the guns. Her present and future are held in the image of sharing food round the table with others to regain a sense of community.

Lives in pictures

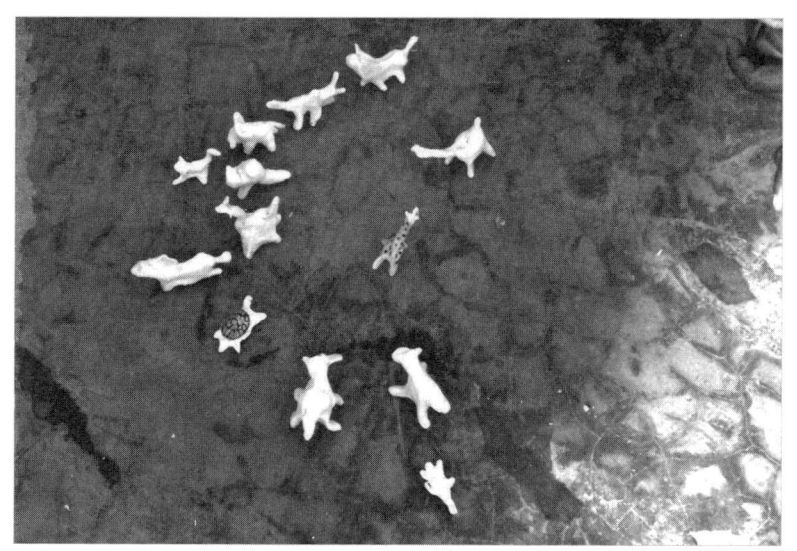

Animals at St Katherine Senior Secondary School, 2012: Expressive arts-based workshop encouraging small group interactions: Participants were put into groups of two or three and asked to create a story about different local animals that they created in soft clay and to imagine a journey with each other. The girls shared stories of the trials and tribulations of meeting friends and foes along the way. Their stories are detailed in Chapter Seven.

9

Women Achievers group and King Solomon Nursery and Primary School

Regina Betty Okwir

> There was no education, no people learning before I began the school that I named King Solomon Nursery and Primary School. ~ Regina Betty Okwir (personal interview, 2013)

We met Betty in 2012 through our friends Esther and Emma. Betty has worked hard to improve the lives of women during and since the LRA war. Headteacher of Ngetta Boys Primary School, she completed her bachelor's degree in Education in 2008. Betty is also devoted to improving the lives of girls and women. To that end, she has created and directed two major projects: Women Achievers Group and the King Solomon Nursery and Primary School. These projects are situated in Ayer Sub-County in Kole District, northern Uganda between Longitudes 32°-34° East and Latitudes 2°-3° North. The district covers a total area of 2.847km^2 with 2.070Km^2 for human settlement, divided into sub-counties.

Here is her story:

I am the head teacher of Ngetta Boys Primary School. For nearly 20 years, peace has been a dream for 1,800,000 people that lived in conflict in northern Uganda. During this time, families lost their children; and adult lives were negatively affected due to the destruction of families, dislocation of entire villages, increased transmission of infections, and disruption of local trading practices, economic livelihoods and livestock elimination from the communities. Social life changed: people were confined to inadequate security around camps in addition to increased poverty, domestic violence, alcoholism and more.

I saw that women needed more empowerment to move forward and succeed. So, I created the Women Achievers Group. The programme is aimed at sensitising women to become self-reliant through small income-generating activities. These programmes help to support households and girls' education using locally available resources through handcrafts. We also help young girls try to become achievers. We also present similar programmes in the villages, and they have understood the importance of girls' education. We include professional women achievers to make presentations at our workshops in order to encourage mothers in rural villages to educate their girls for a better living in the future.

We go as Women Achievers Group to villages and to rural schools to talk to the women from the villages to convince them to keep the girls in schools. We asked them to work together as a team. We also worked together to find ways of surviving through self-reliance. We encouraged the women to find a way out of domestic problems. For instance, they can organise themselves and begin small projects to support them in household activities. Examples include making crafts and using local materials that can earn them a living.

You know, when there is poverty, people are not at peace. So, we advise them to stay together, to do something that can earn them money. That way, they can help their children and their husbands to reduce domestic violence. When there are problems, of course, domestic violence follows.

We also talk to the men. We help them to meet so that they share their ideas. When you talk only to women, the men may come back and say: "Those women are liars." But when they are together, they take the information as a team.

We have very many Women Achievers – over 300, because we have been going from sub-county to sub-county. Sometimes, on market days, we gather them and talk to them. To become a Woman Achiever, you have to show good examples. You have to show your projects. You have to work with other women and pass on information about domestic violence. You send your girl child to school and promote activities to improve society. We now have many women doing that. And they have improved their standard of living. Most of these women started from nothing. And they started sharing their experiences: how they came up from the humble background, from the poverty, together with others in poverty, to gain confidence and move forward.

Each Woman Achiever would develop a topic to share, successful stories to present, in order to help other women. We strive to meet from time to time to encourage one another. They move ahead; they are not at the level we found them. We return to the markets and the villages to support the women, and to see what they are doing.

Some of us try to help young girls become achievers. I have one girl in my home that I picked to become an achiever. She is now at school. We worked with a secondary school as well as a village to help them recognise the importance of girls' education. As we continue, we go to more schools and villages. Sometimes, we go to the market. In this way, we make new starts and we also encourage those who have become Women Achievers.

The story of King Solomon Nursery and Primary School is as follows: I went to buy land for my family. Then, I learned that there was no school around. The nearest primary school was eight kilometres away. The parents from the area where I bought land requested that I start a school there. So, I worked with the community. There was no education, no people learning before I started the school that I named King Solomon Nursery and Primary School.

So, we started under a mango tree. We started with 15 pupils in 2009. Then in 2010, there were 53 pupils. In 2011, there were 130. Now, in 2013, there are 175, from nursery up to Primary Four, with eight teachers. We have the hope that we will continue up to Primary Seven so that we can provide complete primary education. That is how King Solomon Nursery and Primary School started. And when we want women to come for a meeting, to sensitise them, to educate them, we ask school children to take that information to their families.

There is no government support for the school. The parents are poor, but they give something little so that we can continue to develop. To build the school, we asked the parents to bring whatever they could. Some of them would bring a brick or two. Slowly - slowly, we used these materials to construct the buildings. The little money we collect from parents, we give to the teachers. But we hope that as the community grows, more salary payments will be made that we can increase the number of teachers.

We hope that as the King Solomon Nursery and Primary School develops, payment of teachers' salaries will improve; and we shall increase the number of teachers as well. At the moment, the school has benefited the community in the following ways:
- Stopping early marriages and child abuse,
- Reducing defilement, child labour, and domestic violence,
- Encouraging girls to stay at school and increase the number of professional women achievers,
- Discouraging sexual violence, harassment and prostitution,
- Alleviating poverty and improving the standard of living,
- Promoting shared experiences; and
- Training in income-generating activities.

We still have the plan to:
- Build adequate structures for pre-primary and primary education;
- Establish a vocational skills training centre;
- Erect a health unit for healthcare services to address the problem of HIV/AIDs which is currently rampant;
- Conduct outreach programmes as local capacity builders for the communities; and
- Support communities to engage in small income-generation activities to help parents to pay school fees as well as to improve salary payment to teachers in the school.

In these ways, I hope to help the children in the Lango sub-region move towards peace and be prepared for post-war jobs that will help us to develop our community.

10

Community needs – teacher, radio talk show host, and psychologist

Aceng Emma Okite

> My programme is a radio talk show that has addressed various topics, such as domestic violence, post-traumatic stress disorders, child abuse, child sacrifice, gender abuse, rape, defilement, the benefits of educating the girl child, early child marriages, human development and old age, HIV/AIDS and other STDs, among other topics. ~Aceng Emma Okite (personal interview, 2013)

People had little access to television, especially during the war years. Because literacy was low, community radio was the best form of up-to-date reports and information. In the final years of the war, radio programming was used to discuss peace and reconciliation, and to urge abducted children to escape from LRA rebels and return home (Green 2012). Lira has three radio stations: Radio Rhino, Radio Wa, and Quality FM. Radio Rhino was founded by a Ugandan, Pastor Jackson Senyonga, who, during the war, lived outside of Uganda. Radio Wa was started by the Catholic Church, Lira Diocese, and opened by Father John Frazer. He has since returned to Italy, but left the station under the guidance of the Catholic Diocese. Its main purpose is to present Christian messages and to inform listeners about many issues since the time that the LRA war was at its peak. Radio Wa hosts important programmes both for women and the youth. Finally, Quality FM – "Q FM" – is a newly founded radio station that was opened in July 2012 by Okello Kenneth. It is non-denominational.

Aceng Emma Okite hosts community programmes on both Radio Rhino and QFM. This chapter describes Emma's work to found and continue the Gender Programme on Radio Rhino as well as the Community Connection on QFM. Additionally, Emma is well known as an excellent teacher at St Katherine Secondary School, and she recently founded a social work organisation to help community members, called PsychoAid International. She narrates her work as follows:

* * *

I am a psychologist, a teacher, a mother of four and the Executive Director of PsychoAid International Counselling Centre. I had a humble beginning, and many challenged my father for supporting my education, because I was a girl. Being the first daughter and first-born of my late father, the Rev. John Baptist Otim, I was privileged to further my education amidst challenges from my uncles, aunts and clan members who wanted me to be married off at an early age to a very mature man. Fortunately, my father was single-handedly supportive to my education, and he challenged our relatives about the benefits of educating girl children, even though few girls were attending schools at that time. Being a religious person, my father opened our home to many visitors, including people we did not know, and this motivated me to have a heart of compassion, especially to the marginalised.

Before his death, my father told his children always to keep the doors to our homes open to visitors of all categories; not to discriminate, but treat people equally, as God would reward us. I remember him saying the following: "To my beloved children, follow what I have in my will..; no child should remain illiterate...; all the girls in my family, including my granddaughters in the future who come after I have gone to be with the Lord should be educated, plus generations to come" (my late father's will, pages 1-2, 1995). This inspired me to be who I am today, because my father believed in educating girl-children. That is also why I have pledged that through Psycho Aid International, girls and women of Lango sub-region must be educated. My father also motivated me to create the radio programmes during the two decades that women of Lango sub-region were suffering in camps.

Radio Rhino: The gender programme

Radio Rhino, 96.1 Rhino FM, is located in the town centre of Lira District. The station opened in 2000. Not until 2006 did Radio Rhino offer a programme addressing women's issues and problems in the communities.

2006 was also the year that I graduated from Uganda Christian University Mukono with a master's degree in counselling psychology. I wanted to pay back the communities of Lira District and northern Uganda, as a whole, with the knowledge that I had acquired in counselling so that they may have some hope for the future. The northern Uganda LRA war that forced the people of Lira District to abandon their homes and stay in camps was also what inspired me to go for a counselling degree in 2004.

In 2006, I contacted the management of Radio Rhino and shared with them my personal views and ideas about sensitising community members who were by then staying in camps under appalling conditions and were facing multiple life challenges. The response of the Managing Director, Mr Okello Kenneth, was instrumental in starting this radio talk show. The show was called the "Gender Programme," and it addressed issues facing mostly women and girls in the communities. As the programme developed, people advised us to include challenges facing men as well.

I began the Gender Programme on Radio Rhino in 2007, and was later joined by Ekel Margret who was a nursing officer at Lira Regional Hospital. I have also worked with two male moderators since Margret left the show. My programme is a radio talk show that has addressed various topics, such as domestic violence, post-traumatic stress disorders, child abuse, child sacrifice, gender abuse, rape, defilement, the benefits of educating the girl-child, early child marriages, human development and old age, HIV/AIDS and other STDs, among other topics. This programme has created an impact on the lives of the people, not only in Lira District, but northern Uganda and Uganda, as whole. This programme has also transformed the lives of the girls in Lira District and has given hope to the hopeless, as one of the girls, Dorcus, a graduate from Muni National Teachers College said:

I got encouraged. Hope came into my life; and a new future started building up as I listened to the Rhino Radio Gender Programme. I came from Loro in Oyam District. I suffered from domestic violence and early child marriage but was saved and encouraged by Madam Emma's gender programme.

> I took courage one day and went up to Rhino Radio Station and inquired more about Imat Emma, as the listeners called her. Station staff gave me her telephone number. Immediately, I called her and she directed me to her home. When I arrived, she welcomed me and treated me as her own daughter. She supported me and got for me a placement at Muni National Teachers College where I studied for two years and graduated as a Grade Five secondary school teacher. I say thanks to Emma and to Radio Rhino's Gender Programme (interview with Dorcus).

Origins of the gender programme

Many factors contributed to the creation of this programme. Most important was the northern Uganda conflict, which had changed the lives of women and girl children – reducing them to nothing. Already, our culture considered women to be second-class citizens; the northern Uganda war made it worse. Two decades of war caused women in the Lango sub-region to feel hopeless; and tending to their daily living was very difficult. Families started breaking apart. Many of the married men started abandoning their families and wives in favour of prostitutes or other people's wives, since camp life could not give them privacy to fulfil what they believed were their conjugal rights.

A majority of people were exposed to many risky lifestyles and behaviours. The effects were experienced either through domestic violence, separation, and/or abandoning children. As a result, many children went to the streets and survived by either stealing from people, begging, or being employed as porters, hawkers, houseboys, or house girls. When caught stealing, it was not uncommon for business owners to kill the offending child.

Life in camps became increasingly difficult as people's homes became part of the battlefield for Kony's army. Husbands' and wives' lives became ever more stressful and violent. They began hating each other to the extent of killing each other or committing suicide. Domestic violence increased, and so did child abuse. I started my radio talk show to educate the listeners and to teach better ways to manage the stress in their lives. I hosted guests from different backgrounds to discuss topics of their expertise. Sometimes, experienced older women would handle topics such as teaching women peaceful behaviours and management of their homes. One message was to persevere, even in extreme conditions of war. At times, I also hosted men to speak about contentious issues between themselves and women – encouraging discourse between the genders. I also brought children and youth who were being mistreated onto the show, in order to inform the public about shameful behaviours of adults towards children.

After an hour of live presentation talk show, phone lines are opened and listeners call in to ask questions relating to the discussed topics. Guests and I answer the questions or provide clarifications. Sometimes, I give my personal telephone number after the talk show, and listeners can make appointments with me about their personal problems that could not be discussed on air. The talk show runs from 11 am-noon every Sunday, and listeners are not only from Lira District, but the whole of northern and part of the eastern regions.

Impacts of the gender programme

The Gender Programme has helped women and other survivors to tell their own stories. Frequently, these are dreadful experiences. One survivor described how an LRA soldier cut her lips with his knife – exposing her to disease and pain. Another woman confessed that a rebel's actions caused her suffering, pain and rejection by her husband. "The women say that attacks by Lord's Resistance Army rebels have left them with long-term effects and they cannot engage in hard work" (personal interview). My talk show acknowledged that the two-decade war ravaged the Lango sub-region, resulting in gross violations of human rights and loss of lives. At the same time, the Radio Rhino talk show gave hope to the people of Lira District, and lives started changing slowly.

Many people have benefited directly from this radio talk show. Listeners have told me that their lives have been transformed; their families rehabilitated, and those rejected as outcasts from their communities have been accepted and re-integrated. Men and families who rejected and abandoned their lives have told me of their rehabilitation, as well as some women who had run away from their families. Misguided youth who were drug addicts and girls who had joined the streets as sex workers have received counselling, felt empowered, and gained life skills that can better their lives. Parents have learned their responsibility to their children and reduced their abuse of children.

In general, I wanted to give voluntary service to the suffering communities of Lango sub-region and northern Uganda as a whole. I wanted to offer an opportunity to share with the people's pain and suffering resulting from the war. Eventually, this radio talk show became a turning point in many listeners' lives as well as my own.

The programme and its followers have grown. It is popular because it both provides an opportunity to hear about and to ask questions and provide viewpoints about many important topics in our society, some of which are not typically discussed because they are controversial. It has attracted guests such as Apio Vicky Stella, who is a social worker and a counsellor with PsychoAid International. Acar Odit and Thomas Odongo, church leaders, are among others who came to talk on the radio and are now part of the show.

New developments: Q FM and the community connection

Due to the popularity of the Gender Programme, I was encouraged to start a second, longer talk show on Q FM Radio to provide more needs of the community. Community Connection is a two-hour programme that airs on Sunday evenings from 6-8 pm. The show is similar to the Gender Programme, in that it is a talk show that begins with discussion on a topic and may include guest speakers. Near the end, the show is opened to listeners' comments and questions. Topics are not limited to gender topics but include any topics of concern to the community. A programme in July 2013 included Jody McBrien and her husband, Dick Stammer, during which we discussed the challenges of aging and retirement in Uganda.

Both the Gender Programme and Community Connection have helped to mend people's hearts after devastating life situations that resulted from the LRA War. As a result, I was motivated to start an NGO with friends who joined together on my radio show. They are Apio Vicky Stella, a counsellor and social worker; Irene Anamu, a social worker and a counsellor at Lira Regional Referral Hospital; Ocen Tom Moses, a counsellor and a teacher; and myself. Our organisation is called "PsychoAid International." We counsel people from all walks of life: the youth, male and female adults, HIV/AIDS victims and sufferers of domestic abuse, among others. We provide psychosocial support and rehabilitation. This "new-born baby," PsychoAid International, was born as a result of the Radio

Rhino Gender Programme because listeners asked for people who could rehabilitate them and give them a sense of direction, especially the women and girl-children who are the most vulnerable groups, together with the youth who have derailed.

In conclusion, the Radio Rhino Gender Programme has created a great impact on people's lives, especially in Lira District, the Lango sub-region, and northern Uganda as a whole. I offer my gratitude to the managers of Radio Rhino, the many guests who have offered their expert advice and to the listeners of the show.

PsychoAid International

I have been a history teacher at St Katherine's School for Girls for many years. During that time, I have noted the psychosocial issues of the girls caused by the war and other issues, such as poverty. I have striven to help the girls as best I can, including providing them with food, transportation, clothing and counselling.

As a resident of Lira, I have been cognisant of the many psychological needs of community members in town. The pressing need for psychological services led me to create PsychoAid International, which is a charity organisation in Lira District, designed to help people who have war-related psychological issues, as well as other emotional issues related to domestic and other issues in our community. Apart from offering counselling services, PsychoAid International also helps drop-out girls and boys realise their potentials by supporting them through vocational training such as tailoring, needle work, baking, educational support and community transformation through families. For boys who dropped out of school and drug addicts, PsychoAid also provides opportunities to learn carpentry.

11

Cold water: From regional to international documents, and the future women and girls of Lira

Jody McBrien and Julia Byers

"The woman must be restored to her rightful place, as the strong, loving maternal leader of peace and reason." ~ Bryant McGill (2012)

The words and the artistry of Lira women and girls revealed in these pages demonstrate their struggles, pain, resistance, and hopes for more safe, productive and positive lives than they have experienced in past decades. Their grassroots work is essential to bringing about such change. However, support from regional through international policies need both to be in place and to be implemented to facilitate lasting changes to reduce educational gender inequities and to promote rights for women. In this chapter, we will explore local, national and international covenants and agendas designed to bring about more gender equality and relate them to the initiatives of work by Emma, Betty, Grace, Consy, Eunice, and others represented throughout this book.

In December 2012, a Lango Conference in Lira brought together clan leaders from throughout the Lango sub-region to compile the *Te Kwaro Me Lango: Lango Region Development Agenda* (LDA). The Chair of the Steering Committee was Michael M. Odongo; Head of Programmes Sub-Committee, Robert M. Okello; and Lead Reviewer, Joseph Opio Odongo. Emma brought this document to us to demonstrate initiatives developed in the reconstitution and recovery of people in the region. The preamble of the LDA agenda (Odongo, Okello, and Odongo 2012) identifies the Lango people, or Langi, who live in the Lango sub-region north of Lake Kyoga in Uganda. This sub-region is currently comprised of Amolatar, Alebtong, Apac, Dokolo, Kole, Lira, Oyam and Otuke districts.

The agenda provides a history of the local chiefs and tribes and acknowledges the ways in which the British colonialism disrupted local communal ways of life. The Langi constitute a population of over two million and are the sixth major nationality in Uganda. The majority of the two million are ages 15-30 years old. The clan's poverty rate is nearly 60 per cent vs. 34 per cent nationally, and the child mortality rate is 177 vs. 134 per thousand. Primary school enrolment is also worse than the national average, at 47.1 per cent vs. 57.4 per cent; and the HIV prevalence is 8.3 per cent vs. 6.4 per cent. These and other factors indicate that this region is in need of conscious developments to help restore and re-invigorate both the spirit and the means of living an improved quality of life.

In Part II of the LDA, the strategic framework to mobilise the community aims to define, in a participatory and grassroots manner, the future of the region. The vision is to have a "united, strong and prosperous Lango community assuming its rightful place in a united and peaceful Uganda." Its mission is "to promote social and economic welfare of Lango households." Langi values include: "respect and dignity, hard work, independence, honesty, equality and equity" (p.6). Part III focuses on strategic objectives to accomplish the goals of the overall framework. The leaders agreed that strengthening traditional leadership and cultural values can define the identity, spirit and sense of direction for a society. The "P.O. Box" and "Dot Com" generations have deeply influenced the social networks of Lango people, while the values and resilience of clan members need constant addressing.

From this perspective, the views of the women expressed in our book aim to qualitatively influence their society's dream for the future. In this pursuit, however, they are frequently obstructed by the history of patriarchy in Uganda and the Lango culture. The *Te Kwaro Me Lango* states: "Culture can be said to be the operating field of cultural leadership because it defines and delimits the manner in which cultural leadership operates" (p. 9). Perhaps still entrenched within locals is the fact that cultural leadership in the past has been primarily male dominated. After 40 years of civil wars and disruptions, since the time of Amin, the current leadership needs to move from war leadership to one in which leaders drive the population towards economic and cultural development and the accruing transformation. Until very recently, in part due to the decades of war, top decision-making bodies were delegated, or rather taken over by men. "Youths, women, people with disabilities and all other vulnerable groups were not considered for such positions, with the result that their views, needs and opinions were left out in clan policy-making bodies" (p. 12).

The 1995 Constitution and other legal frameworks of Uganda laid the foundation for the "recognition, revival, and operation of a reformed cultural leadership that practises the core principles contained in International Treaties, Conventions, Regional Instruments and National Policies" (Odongo, Okello, and Odongo 2012, p.14). This meant that focus would be on strengthening the system by giving women, the youth, the elderly and people with disabilities a much larger voice. In this way, decisions that are responsive to the needs of the whole community are honoured with dignity and respect. The Lango Cultural Foundation, registered as an NGO, was created. There are expectations that women and the youth be represented in all the assignments of functions and powers, but the General Assembly still struggles with the composition and roles of leadership.

The Lango Development Agenda aims to utilise new, positive global practices. Composition of the leadership of the Lango Region requires a diversity of all ages, eighteen years and above, with educational background, skills and other competencies with the necessity of the inclusion of women, youth and people with disabilities. The Lango ethnic group has been described as an egalitarian society where the community is key and the individual tends to be considered secondarily to the whole. When someone achieves an education and rises above the community norms, in most cases, achievers are punished, directly or indirectly. Women especially can be shunned and attempts are made to diminish their success. Yet, if an individual has persevered and overcome negative forces, her achievement tends to be seen as an achievement of the community. She is expected to give back and to provide clothes, food, money and service to her community.

Hard work used to be a characteristic of the Lango culture. There was never famine, poverty, or homelessness until the violence and disruption of family life occurred during the wars. Displaced people lacked the support of communal life and many became despondent and void of any sense of direction since the collective growth of the community was disbanded and traumatised. At the same time, positive aspects of the Lango people include the "forgiving spirit, kindness and gentleness" that we experienced in visiting and working with the women and girls of Lira.

With the Poverty Eradication of 2004, the Uganda National Culture Policy (2006), and the Cross Cultural Foundation of Uganda (CCFU), organisations have pressed the government to prioritise and infuse culture in development initiatives, and to "earmark at least one per cent of the national budget to cultural development programs" (p.24). Arts and crafts, folklore and even global markets for herbal products are seen as a wave of the future. The Children of

Hope Uganda, Te-cwao, and other initiatives highlight local support for this initiative.

Health and fertility rates comprise other gender issues that the community must address. According to the report, an estimated 10.1% of women aged 15-49 among the Langi are HIV positive. Their fertility rate is 6.3 children. The high teen pregnancy rate contributes to high school drop-out rates of girls and high mother and infant mortality rates.

Perhaps most important is the encouragement of girls to get a basic education. The LDA recognises the injustices imposed on girls in IDP camps, leading to numerous rapes and forced prostitution (p. 31). It also prioritises girls' education in its strategic objectives. In spite of governmental policies for universal education at primary (UPE) and secondary (USE) levels, *Te Kwaro Me Lango* recognises a great gulf between the policies and actual practices regarding girls' education throughout Uganda. Statistics expressed include the following:

- Only 21 per cent of girls attend secondary school.
- 20 per cent are married before their 20th birthday.
- 35 per cent are mothers before their 18th birthday.

Currently, as stated before, it takes an average of US$25 to send a girl to school for a term. Due to extreme poverty, many girls are kept at home to care for younger siblings or maintain the family work. Many girls walk several miles a day to bring water to their families. As mentioned earlier, Uganda has a goal to make this distance no more than one and a half kilometres. Ideally, this begins to free girl-children to attend school. Tribes delegate the job of gathering water for the community not to the wife, husband, or son, but to the girl-child. This tradition greatly reduces opportunities for girls to receive an education. The future and hope for Lira and the surrounding towns in the region and Uganda, as a whole, may indeed be dependent on "cold water." The riches of water may be priceless to the reconstitution of the body, mind and spirit of the future cultural leaders.

Major international conventions and goals supporting equality for women and girls are found in the UN Convention on the Elimination of all Forms of Discrimination against Women (CEDAW), which Uganda ratified in 1985; the UN Convention on the Rights of the Child, ratified by Uganda in 1990; and the UN Millennium Development Goals (MDGs). Countries that ratify CEDAW commit themselves to legal and judicial policies that abolish discriminatory laws and policies against women and to eliminating individual and systemic forms of discrimination against women. Article 3 requires States to create measures that allow for the advancement of women in political, social, economic and cultural fields. Nations are to "modify the social and cultural patterns of the conduct of men and women, with a view to achieving the elimination of prejudices and customary and all other practices which are based on the idea of the inferiority or the superiority of either of the sexes or on stereotyped roles for men or women" (CEDAW, Article 6). Other articles call for career and vocational equal training and opportunities, employment opportunities, equal access to educational opportunities and facilities, sufficient healthcare, choice in pregnancies and guardianship of children, and more. Provisions in the 2012 LDA recognise these issues and purport to change past policies and practices to better welcome women into leadership positions as well as increased opportunities for education.

Articles from the UN Convention on the Rights of the Child include rights that children not be separated from parents against their will (Article 9); that children can express their thoughts freely (Article 13); that they be protected from physical or mental violence, including sexual violence (Article 19); that they enjoy health and protection (Articles 24-27); and that they have rights to education, including free primary schooling. As witnessed from the narratives and artwork by the women and girls of Lira, issues of mental and physical violence must be taken seriously to advance their rights. Additionally, girls need additional supports that will encourage their parents to keep them in school. Children who are taken by their fathers upon separation/divorce must also be protected and allowed to maintain time with their mothers, or to choose to live with their mothers without punishment. They also need protection through laws that are followed strictly to protect them from rape, unintended pregnancy and HIV/AIDS, as well as the allowance for their continued education.

The first six out of the eight MDGs are linked to advancement of women in northern Uganda:

- Eradicate extreme poverty and hunger;
- Achieve universal primary education;
- Promote gender equality and empower women;
- Reduce child mortality;
- Improve maternal health; and
- Combat HIV/AIDS, malaria and other diseases.

Poverty has repeatedly been noted as a factor that reduces girls' and women's opportunities in Lira. Percentages of girls at school were noted as low in the Lango sub-region, as compared to the country as a whole. Gender equality and empowerment of women, while advancing, need far more support. Workshops conducted with men and with mixed genders in the sub-region are making progress, but such projects must be increased and sustained, in order to help both men and women understand that females deserve equal respect. The practice of selling young girls into marriage to gain a bride price must be discouraged, perhaps with laws enforcing minimum ages and bride prices. Girls forced to wed pre-puberty or in early stages of adolescence are far more likely to die in childbirth and/or to lose their unborn children in miscarriages.

Finally, not only CBOs and NGOs, but the Ugandan government, need to make a commitment to the reduction of HIV/AIDS, malaria and other life-devastating illnesses that can be reduced through education and medication. The government needs to make these health issues a priority in the national budget by increasing well-supplied health clinics throughout rural areas.

We see these priorities in the work of our Lira colleagues. Through the Women Achievers programme, Okwir Betty Regina and others are working to reduce poverty; increase education; empower women; and bolster communication between women and men. Betty has also worked tirelessly in the pursuit of universal primary education through opening and maintaining the King Solomon Nursery and Primary School on a shoestring budget. Akwang Eunice has doubled the size of the Te-cwao co-op , with plans to extend projects, markets, and trainings. Her efforts result in more children attending school. Aceng Emma Okite has provided mental healthcare for a community in need through PsychoAid International. Additionally, she has provided professional advice and support to the community through her radio programmes, and she has mentored girls through her work as a teacher and counsellor at St Katherine's School for Girls. Kia Betty works for social justice in her role as a government official and a volunteer in Women Achievers Group. Ogwal Consy dedicates time to helping abducted children return and rehabilitate. Her formerly abducted daughter, Acan Grace, now works with formerly abducted women to provide resources that can help them move on and succeed in their lives.

The day before returning home from our March 2012 travels to Lira, we joined with hundreds of women and girls to celebrate the UN International Women's Day in Ugandan style. It was a bright day, both metaphorically and literally. Only a canopy tent and cold water bottles given to the audience cooled the heat of the sun. The event took place in the large public field in the centre of Lira. We watched the elder women dressed in beautiful traditional Ugandan costumes juxtaposed against the dry, gritty earth below our feet. The tailored emphasis of the women's metallic, unique dresses were the tall shoulder pads, which gave the illusion that their bodies included brightly coloured wings.

Across the field from these women were more women, dressed in military regalia with red berets, thick leather belts, industrial black boots and tan uniforms. The elders danced in a circle – the colourful fabric of their dresses swirling in the sun. The soldiers marched in a disciplined line, raising their guns and tipping their hats to the dignitaries as they walked by. Filling the space between the elders and the soldiers were rows and rows of schoolgirls in their school uniforms of blue, bright orange and brown, parading across the terrace, marching military style. They paused to honour the dignitaries in the canopy tent, then continued marching – some so genuinely focused on mastering the military kick walk that several shoes flew off and darted into the air. There were quick giggles and several of the bystander children ran to pick up the abandoned shoes while the girls marched ceremoniously on.

Invited to join the dignitaries, we sat in shade of the canopy tent. In a show of solidarity with the Ugandan women who had so graciously welcomed us, Jody wore an African dress and Julia showcased her African-style braided hair. In the middle of the regal ceremonies, we watched as one young girl, oblivious to the general fanfare, randomly walked across the staging area. We looked at each other and grinned. The stunning pre-school girl wore a brilliant white celebratory dress that contrasted with her gleaming black skin and she carried a water bottle as she meandered across the field. Not sure of where she was going, the collective protection of many motherly onlookers gently reached out to find her mother. We all expressed relief when we realised the mother was indeed nearby. Eventually, the child returned and curled up on her mother's lap, clutching the water bottle as she continued to watch the show. More parades of women and girls, along with speeches by Lira women, lasted for hours into the heat of the day, as we observed and felt the importance of this moment. We later remarked that Uganda makes this UN Day a national holiday, closing non-essential services in order to celebrate. In contrast, in the US, only a small percentage of the population is even aware of the March date.

What struck us the most about that memorable day in Lira was the memory of that confident little girl clutching her water bottle. Feeling both protected yet fiercely independent, she is emblematic of hope for the future of this town, and indeed, for Uganda. The girl-child straddled the ground between a military presence and celebratory group working to make changes to traditions in order to empower girls and women. Indeed, the fact that women were in the military exemplified changes in centuries of male-dominated traditions. But ultimately, the girl symbolised the heart of our multi-year work with the women and girls of Lira, Uganda. Given these options, war or peace, equality or patriarchy, in which direction will the country proceed? The determination and sacrifice of the women and girls, as well as many men, give us hope that the country will advance towards a more equitable and peaceful nation, as long as the women continue to find support and break new ground as demonstrated in these pages.

Suggested resources

This resource chapter includes various forms of media to help readers learn more about children and families living through conflict, with particular regard to Uganda and women's and children's issues.

Books

Ainebyona, G. (2011) *The Reintegration of Female Ex-Abductees of the Lord's Resistance Army: A Case of Gulu District.* Saarbrücken: Lambert Academic Publishing.

Apio, L. (2012) *LRA Conflict – Impact and Women's Peace Efforts in Northern Uganda: The Impact of the Lord's Resistance Army War on Women and Women's Efforts towards Peace in Northern Uganda.* Saarbrücken: Lambert Academic Publishing.

Cook, K. (2009) *Stolen Angels: The Kidnapped Girls of Uganda.* Toronto: Penguin Canada.

Dallaire, C. *They Fight like Soldiers, They Die like Children.* Toronto: Random House Canada.

De Temmerman, E. (1995) *Aboke Girls: Children Abducted in Northern Uganda.* Kampala: Fountain Publishers.

Dunson, D. H. (2008) *Child, Victim, Soldier: The Loss of Innocence in Uganda.* Maryknoll, New York: Orbis Books.

Jagieski, W. W. (2012) *The Night Wanderers: Uganda's Children and the Lord's Resistance Army.* New York: Seven Stories Press.

Kwesiga, J. C. (2002) *Women's Access to Higher Education in Africa: Uganda.* Kampala: Fountain Publishers.

London, C. (2007) *Voices of Children in War: One Day the Soldiers Came.* New York: HarperCollins.

McDonnell, F.J., and Akal.G. (2007) *Girl Soldier: A Story of Hope for Northern Uganda's Children.* Ada: Chosen Books.

Oloya, Opiyo (2013) *Child to Soldier: Stories from Joseph Kony's Lord's Resistance Army.* Toronto: University of Toronto Press.

Phoung,P., Vinck, P., and Eric S. (2007) *Abducted: The Lord's Resistance Army and Forced Conscription in Northern Uganda.* Berkeley-Tulane Initiative on Vulnerable Populations. Accessed at http://hhi.harvard.edu/sites/default/files/publications/publications%20-%20evaluation%20-%20abducted.pdf

Tripp, A. M. (2000) *Women and Politics in Uganda*. Kampala: Fountain Publishers.
Tripp, A. M., and Kwesiga. J.C.(2002) *The Women's Movement in Uganda: History, Challenges, and Prospects*. Kampala: Fountain Publishers.

Films

Invisible Children. Invisiblechildren.com. This organisation has created numerous documentary films about Kony and the LRA.
Krakower, A. (2010) *The Children's War*. Cinema Libre Studio.
Sewing Hope: The Story of Sister Rosemary Nyirumbe. (2014) See sewinghope.com
Yoeli, B. (Director). (2012) *After Kony: Staging hope*. Gravitas Ventures, LLC.

Organisations

AVCOH (Alternative to Violence Centered Organisation for Humanity). As mentioned in the introduction, this organisation works to increase awareness and support for women's rights and psychosocial development and to improve the life skills of women with the goal of empowering communities to create a foundation for long-term economic security and to promote peace and development. AVCOH is a CBO registered since 2009 to implement government health programmes to alleviate problems in health and human rights, especially in the areas of HIV/AIDS and water safety. The headquarters is located at Plot 17, Maruzi Road, Lira. To learn more or to contribute to the organisation, please email avcohorg@yahoo.com.

Centre for Children in Vulnerable Situations (CCVS): CCVS is a Belgian research centre that maintains partnerships with three Belgian universities. Its goal is to promote psychosocial wellbeing of children and youth who live in vulnerable situations in various countries. One of its sites is in Lira, Uganda. Learn more at http://www.centreforchildren.be.

Forum for African Women's Educationalists (FAWE): This continent-wide group has a chapter in Uganda. Its many activities include the following: participation in the Ministry of Education's National Taskforce on gender, participation in reviewing bylaws for child protection, campaigning to recruit more female science teachers, training teachers in gender responsive pedagogy, radio campaigns on girls' education, involvement and membership in the United Nations Girls' Education Initiative (UNGEI), and providing role models to encourage and support girls' education. More information is available at http://www.fawe.org/.

Freidis Rehabilitation and Disabled Centre, Lira: While traveling in the Lango sub-region in 2002, Christopher Jogole and his Norwegian wife, Freidis Person, noted the need for a centre to rehabilitate and reintegrate women, war victims, and children with disabilities. Freidis Rehabilitation and Disable Centre (FRDC) was inaugurated in 2007 by President Museveni, and it is a registered non-governmental organisation (NGO) located in Lira. The Centre strives to contribute to the physical and psychosocial recovery of children with disabilities, orphans, war-affected, and other vulnerable children. For more information and to contribute to this organisation, please visit http://www.frdc.no/.

Invisible Children: Founded in 2004 by Jason Russell, Invisible Children works to inform the public about LRA atrocities; protect communities attacked by the LRA; recover and rehabilitate children abducted by the LRA; and mobilise groups to advance international activity to capture Joseph Kony and end LRA violence. They offer numerous campaigns, resources, films and products made by rehabilitated child soldiers to help the young people earn a living wage. Their website is http://www.invisiblechildren.com; and they have a Facebook page at https://www.facebook.com/invisiblechildren.

PsychoAid International: Emma Okite is the Founder and Executive Director of this organisation that supports the mental health and wellbeing of community members, with an emphasis on women and girls' education and psychosocial wellbeing. PsychoAid helps both girls and boys realise their potential by supporting them through academic and vocational training such as tailoring, needlework, baking and carpentry. For more information and to contribute, please contact PsychoAid International, P.O. Box 1052, Lira, Uganda. Email: psychoaidinternational@yahoo.com or emmaokite@yahoo.com. The Centre needs and accepts donations.

Te-cwao: Akwang Eunice is the Director of this CBO, which helps women create jewellery, baskets and other products for purchase. Te-cwao also works to provide community members with other livelihoods through agricultural projects. The organisation is in great need of funding. To contribute to this cause, please email Eunice at tecwao@yahoo.com

Scholarly publications

Auger, R. W. (2004) "What We Don't Know CAN Hurt Us: Mental Health Counselors' Implicit Assumptions about Human Nature". *Journal of Mental Health Counseling,* 26 (1), 13-24.

Byers, J., and Gere.S. (2007) "Expression in the Service of Humanity: Trauma and Temporality". *Journal Of Humanistic Psychology,* 47 (3), 384-391.

Cattaneo, M (1994) "Addressing Culture and Values in the Training of Art Therapists. *Art Therapy,* 11(3), 184-186.

Chang, M. "Cultural Consciousness and the Global Context of Dance/Movement Therapy". In Chaiklin,S., and Wengrower,H. (Eds.) (2009) *The Art and Science of Dance/Movement Therapy: Life is Dance,* 299-316. New York: Routledge/Taylor & Francis Group.

Constantine, M.G. and Sue, D.W. (Eds). (2006) *Addressing Racism: Facilitating Cultural Competence in Mental Health and Educational Settings*. New York: John Wiley & Sons.

Freire, P. (1998) *Pedagogy of the Oppressed*. New York: Continuum.

Gilligan, C., Rogers, A.G., and Tolman, D.L. (Eds).(1991) *Women, Girls and Psychotherapy: Reframing Resistance*. New York: The Haworth Press.

Heller, J. (2010) "Emerging Themes on Aspects of Social Class and the Discourse of White Privilege." *Journal of Intercultural Studies*, 31(1), 111-120.

Johnson, A.G. (2005) *Privilege, Power and Difference* (2nd ed). New York: McGraw Hill Humanities.

Jones, C., F. B., and Day, T. (2004) "From Healing Rituals to Music Therapy: Bridging the Cultural Divide between Therapist and Young Sudanese Refugees." *The Arts and Psychotherapy*, 31(2), 89-100.

Kapitan, L. (2004) "Global Perspective of Practice." *Art Therapy*, 23 (2), 50-51.

La Roche, M. J. and Maxie, A. (2003) "Ten Considerations in Addressing Cultural Differences in Psychotherapy." *Professional Psychology: Research and Practice*, 34 (2), 180-186.

McBrien, J.L., Betty A. Ezati, and Jan Stewart, J. "Young women and survival in post-war: Experiences of secondary school girls in Uganda." In C. R. Rodriguez, D. Tsikata, & A. A. Amposo (Eds.) (2015), *Transatlantic feminisms*, 213-234. Lanham: Roman & Littlefield.

McBrien, J. L., and Day. R. (2012) "From There to Here: Using Photography to Explore Acculturation with Resettled Refugee Youth." *International Journal of Child, Youth, and Family Studies*, 3 (4.1), 546-568.

McBrien, J. L. (2011) "The importance of context: Vietnamese, Somali, and Iranian refugee mothers discuss their resettled lives and involvement in their children's education." *Compare, 4* , 75-90.

Macintyre, A. "The Virtues, the Unity of a Human Life, and the Concept of a Tradition." Hinchman and Hinchman, S. (Eds) 1997 in *Memory, Identity, and Community: the Idea of Narrative in the Human Sciences*, 254-257. Albany, State University of New York.

Paulson, J. (Ed.) (2011) *Education, Conflict and Development*. Oxford: Symposium Books. [Part Three of this book addresses Northern Uganda.]

Pedersen, P., J. G. Draguns, W. J. Lonner, and (2008) Trimble, J.E. (Eds). *Counselling across Cultures*. Thousand Oaks, CA: Sage Publication.

Pedersen, P. B., Crethar, H.C., and J. Carlson.J. (2008) "Toward More Inclusive Empathy: A Survey of Relational Worldviews and Alternative Modes of Helping." In P. B. Pedersen, Crethar, H.C., and Carlson (Eds.), *Inclusive Cultural Empathy: Making Relationships Central in Counselling and Psychotherapy* (1st ed.). Washington, DC: American Psychological Association.

Rousseau, C., M.,Gauthier, B.M.,L., Alain, .N.L., Rojas,V., Moran, A., and Bourassa, D. (2007) "Classroom Drama Therapy Program for Immigrant and Refugee Adolescents: A Pilot Study." *Clinical Child Psychology & Psychiatry*, 12 (3),451-465.

Steele, W., and Malchiodi,C.A. (2012) *Trauma Informed Practices with Children and Adolescents*. New York: Taylor & Francis Group.

Stewart, J., Kuly, M., Ezati, B., and McBrien,J.L. "The Importance of Storytelling for Peace-Building in Post-Conflict States." In Finley, L., Connors,J., and Wien,B. (Eds.). (2015) *Teaching Peace through Popular Culture*. Information Age Press.

Sue, D. W. "The Invisible Whiteness of Being." In Constantine,M.G., and Sue,D.W., (Eds.). (2006) *Addressing Racism: Facilitating Cultural Competence in Mental Health and Educational Settings*, 15-30. New York: John Wiley & Sons.

Sue, D.W. and D. Sue.(2007) *Counselling the Culturally Different: Theory and Practice* (5th ed). New York: John Wiley & Sons.

References

Alfonso, G.A., and Byers. J.G. "Art Therapy and Disaster Relief in the Philippines.". In J. S. Potash, S. M. Chan, and D. L. Kalmanowitz (Eds). (2012) *Art Therapy in Asia: To the Bone or Wrapped in Silk*. Philadelphia: Jessica Kingsley Publishers.

American Anthropological Association. (1947) "Statement of Human Rights." *American Anthropologist,* 49 (4), 539-543.

Ayebazibwe, A. (2013, July 11). "Teenage Pregnancy: A Big Threat to Uganda's Girl-Child." *The Daily Monitor*, p. 1. Accessed August 14, 2013, at http://www.monitor.co.ug/News/National/Teenage-pregnancy--The-pain-of-child-mothers/-/688334/1910850/-/h55g0dz/-/index.html

Besic, J., and McBrien J.L. (2012). "Crossing International and Research Boundaries: From Subject to Author for an Authentic Refugee Portrait.*" International Scholarly Research Network* (IRSN) *Education Journal,* 2012, Article ID 830938.

Byers, J. G., and Gere.S.H. (2007) "Expression in the Service of Humanity: Trauma and Temporality. *Journal of Humanistic Psychology*. In 47 (3) , 384-391. Doi: 10.1177/0022167807302186.

Calhoun, L. G., A. Cann,A and Tedeschi.R.G. "The Posttraumatic Growth Model: Sociocultural Considerations." T. Weiss & R. Berger (eds.), (2010) *Posttraumatic Growth and Culturally Competent Practice: Lessons Learned from around the Globe*, 1-14. Hoboken: John Wiley & Sons.

CoopAfrica (The Cooperative Facility for Africa, 2013). Empower rural women – end poverty and hunger: The potential of African cooperatives. International Labour Office. Retrieved from http://www.ilo.org/public/english/employment/ent/coop/africa/download/coopafrica_leaflet_iwd2012.pdf

CIA. *The World Factbook*. Accessed August 14, 2013, from https://www.cia.gov/index.html

De Temmerman, E. (1995) *Aboke Girls: Children Abducted in Northern Uganda*. Kampala: Fountain Publishers.

Dolan, C. Collapsing masculinities and weak states – A case study of northern Uganda. In F. Cleaver (Ed.) (2003) Masculinity matters: Men, masculinities and gender in relations to development. London: Zed Books.

Eichstaedt, P. (2009) *First Kill your Family: Child Soldiers of Uganda and the Lord's Resistance Army*. Chicago: Chicago Review Press.

Ellison, M (2006) Rehabilitation and Reintegration of War Affected Children in Northern Uganda. A Project of Sponsoring Children Uganda by the Belgium Government. Accessed August 14, 2013, at http://www.scribd.com/doc/85536014/Rachele-Rehabilitation-Centre-final-report

Ferguson, H., & Kepe, T. (2011). Agricultural cooperatives and social empowerment of women: A Ugandan case study. *Development in Practice*, 21(3), 421-429.

Girls Not Brides. (2012) About Child Marriage. Accessed July 15, 2013, at http://www.girlsnotbrides.org/about-child-marriage.

Gree, A. *UGANDA: Using Community Radio to Heal after Kony's war*. Inter Press Service News Agency. Accessed July 6, 2013, at http://www.ipsnews.net/2012/01/uganda-using-community-radio-to-heal-after-konyrsquos-war/, 2012

International Centre for Transitional Justice (ICTJ, 2014). Confronting impunity and engendering justice processes in northern Uganda. Briefing. Accessed June 21, 2015, at https://www.ictj.org/sites/default/files/ICTJ-Uganda-GenderBriefing-New-2014.pdf

Jaqeilski, W. (2012) *The Night Wanderers: Uganda's Children and the Lord's Resistance Army*. New York: Seven Stories Press.

Justice and Reconciliation Project (JRP 2009) Kill every living thing: The Barlonyo massacre. Accessed June 18, 2015 at http://justiceandreconciliation.com/wp-content/uploads/2009/02/JRP_FN9_Barlonyo-2009.pdf

Kasirye, I. (2011) Addressing gender gaps in the Ugandan labour market. EPRC Policy Brief, no. 12. Accessed June 16, 2015 at http://elibrary.acbfpact.org/acbf/collect/acbf/index/assoc/HASHf1fb.dir/doc.pdf

Lawrence-Lightfoot, S., and Davis, H.H. (1997) *The Art and Science of Portraiture*. Hoboken: Jossey-Bass.

Lira District website. Accessed February 2, 2014, at http://liradistrict.com/.

Malchiodi, C. (2012) *Handbook of Art Therapy* (2nd ed.). New York: The Guilford Press.

McDonnell, F. J., and Akallo, G.(2007) *Girl Soldier: A Story of Hope for Northern Uganda's Children*. Chosen Books.

McCormac, M., & Benjamin, J. A. (2008) Education and fragility in northern Uganda. American Institutes for Research. Accessed June 22, 2015, at http://www.equip123.net/docs/E1-Education_Fragility_Uganda.pdf.

McGill, B. (2012) *Voice of Reason: Speaking to the Great and Good Spirit of Revolution of Mind*. New Dehli: Paper Lyon Publishing.

Mohanty, C. T.(2002) "'Under Western Eyes' Revisited: Feminist Solidarity through Anticapitalist Struggles." *Signs: Journal of Women in Culture and Society*, 28 (2), 499-535.

- "Under Western Eyes: Feminist Scholarship and Colonial Discourses." *Feminist Review*, 30 (1988): 61-88. Accessed January 23, 2012, at http://moodle.intolearning.ie/webdav/EqualEyes/modules/Module4/Mohanty_UnderWesternEyes.pdf

Munuh, T. (2007, November 26) "African Women and Domestic Violence." *50.50 Inclusive Democracy.* Accessed April 15, 2015, at https://www.opendemocracy.net/content/african-women-and-domestic-violence

Noddings, N.(2005) *Challenge to Care in Schools: An Alternative Approach to Education.* New York: Teacher's College Press.

Odongo, M., Okello, R.,and Odongo J. O. (2012) *Te Kwaro Me Lango*, Lira.

Okite, E. "Conversations from "Community Connections." Quality Radio FM, 2012-2013.

Okite, E. "Conversations from the Gender Programme." Radio Rhino, 2004-2013.

Olika, B. H. "Aboke Girls: Looking for Night Achiro." *The Observer* (2013, July 28). Accessed August 1, 2013, at http://observer.ug/index.php?option=com_content&view=article&id=26643:aboke-girls-looking-for-night-achiro

Omona, E. (2012, August 13). "80% of Northern Uganda Youths are Unemployed." *Uganda Picks.* Accessed August 14, 2013, at http://www.ugandapicks.com/2012/08/80-of-northern-uganda-youths-are-unemployed-92433.html

Opiyo, Oloya (2013) *Child to Soldier: Stories from Joseph Kony's Lord's Resistance Army.* Toronto: University of Toronto Press.

Roberts, B., Ocaka, K. F., Browne, J., Oyok, T., and Sondorp, E. (2011) Alcohol disorder amongst forcibly displaced persons in northern Uganda. *Addictive Behaviours*, 36(8), 870-873.

Shiva, V., R. Gordon, and Wing.B. (2000) "Global Brahmanism: The Meaning of the WTO Protests: An Interview with Dr. Vandana Shiva." *Color Lines: Race, Color, Action,* 3 (2), 30–32.

Shiva, V., Asfar, J.H., Bedi, G., and Holla-Bhar. R.(1997) *The Enclosure and Recovery of the Commons: Biodiversity, Indigenous Knowledge, and Intellectual Property Rights.* New Delhi: Research Foundation for Science, Technology, and Ecology.

Siegel, D. (2010) *Mindsight: The New Science of Personal Transformation.* New York: Bantam Books.

Steele, W., and Malchiodi. C.A.(2012) *Trauma Informed Practices with Children and Adolescents,* New York: Taylor & Francis Group.

Synopsis (unpublished). International Women's Day, Lira, Uganda, 2012.

TASO (2012). The AIDS Support System. Accessed April 25, 2013, at http://www.tasouganda.org/

Tebusabwa, M. K. (n.d.; post 2008) Gender inequalities in the value chain of export crop production in Uganda: A case study of cocoa farmers in Bundibugyo district. Council for Economic Empowerment for Women of Africa. Retrieved from https://editorialexpress.com/cgi-bin/conference/download.cgi?db_name=IAFFE2010&paper_id=41

Tedeschi, R. G., and Calhoun.,L.G.(2010). "A Clinical Approach to Posttraumatic Growth." In *Positive psychology in practice*, Linley,P.A.,and Joseph,S. (eds.): 405-419. Hoboken: John Wiley & Sons.

- (1996) "The Posttraumatic Growth Inventory: Measuring the Positive Legacy of Trauma." *Journal of Traumatic Stress*, 9, (3), 455-471.
Temple, B., and Young. A. "Qualitative Research and Translation Dilemmas." *Qualitative Research*, 4(2), 161-178. Doi: 10.1177/1468794104044430
Trilling, Lionel (2008). *The Moral Obligation to be Intelligent: Selected Essays*. Evanston: Northwestern University Press.
Tripp, A. M., and Kwesiga, J.C. (Eds.) (2002) *The Women's Movement in Uganda: History, Challenges, and Prospects*. Kampala: Fountain Publishers.
"Uganda: Domestic Violence, including Legislation, Statistics, and Attitudes toward Domestic Violence; the Availability of Protection and Support Services" (2008). Immigration and Refugee Board of Canada, Ottawa. Accessed November 12, 2012, at http://www.refworld.org/cgi-bin/texis/vtx/rwmain?docid=49b92b20c
Ugandan National Culture Policy (2006).
UNICEF. *The State of the World's Children 2004: Girls, Education and Development*. Accessed January 23, 2013, at http://www.unicef.org/sowc04/index.html
- *The State of the World's Children 2007: Women and Children – The Double Dividend of Gender Equality*. Accessed at http://www.unicef.org/sowc07/index.php
UNHCR (2012). "UNHCR Closes Chapter on Uganda's Internally Displaced People." Accessed September 12, 2013, at http://www.unhcr.org/4f06e2a79.html
UN.org (n.d.) Ten Stories the World Should Hear More About. Accessed at http://www.un.org/events/tenstories/06/story.asp?storyID=100
UN Human Rights (1990) Convention on the Rights of the Child. Accessed at http://www.ohchr.org/en/professionalinterest/pages/crc.aspx
UN Millennium Development Goals (n.d.) Accessed at http://www.un.org/millenniumgoals/poverty.shtml
UN Women (n.d.) Convention on the Elimination of All Forms of Discrimination against Women. Accessed March 12, 2014, at http://www.un.org/womenwatch/daw/cedaw/text/econvention.htm
US Department of State (2012) *The Lord's Resistance Army: Fact Sheet*. Accessed at http://www.state.gov/r/pa/prs/ps/2012/03/186734.htm
US Department of State (2008) "Uganda. Country Reports on Human Rights Practices for 2007."
Uwezo Uganda. *Are our children learning? Annual learning assessment report,* 2011. Accessed at http://www.uwezo.net/wp-content/uploads/2012/08/UG_2011AnnualAssessmentReport.pdf
WELL. "Water and Sanitation in Uganda – Measuring Performance for Improved Service Delivery." Executive summary, 2003. Accessed at http://www.lboro.ac.uk/well/resources/consultancy-reports/wsiu-exec-sum.htm

Women's Commission for Refugee Women and Children. *(2004) No Safe Place to Call Home: Children and Adolescent Night Commuters in Northern Uganda.* New York: Women's Commission for Refugee Women and Children. Accessed Aug_7, 2012, at https://womensrefugeecommission.org/news/press-releases-and-statements/425-no-safe-place-to-call-home-qnight-commutersq-in-northern-uganda-leave-home-to-seek-safety

Woodall, J. (2007) "Suffering, Art, and Healing." *Journal of Pedagogy, Pluralism, and Practice,* 3 (4). Accessed March 12, 2013, at http://www.lesley.edu/journal-pedagogy-pluralism-practice/

Zinn, H. (2006) *A Power Governments Cannot Suppress.* San Francisco: City Lights Publishers.

Kickstarter contributors

Our gratitude to all who contributed to our Kickstarter campaign that provided production coasts for Cold Water. As promised, here is a list of all who contributed $20 or more:

Bryan and Kat Atherton
Richard Stammer
Tom and Kathy Cook
Peter and Grace French
Brock and Julie Leach
Joan and Charlie Cooper
Gary and Kathy Feige
Mark Klisch
Edward Yelochan
Richard Borghesi
JoeAnn Gidlow
Louise King
Gail Clifton
Arthur Guilford
Ross Alander
Graceann Dieterich
Lawry Reid
Carol Turner
Joan Lennon
Patricia Hunsader
Kim Meilke
Lois Natiello
Ashley Metelus
Karen Weber
Gerry and Mary Preston
Leonor Machado
Mary Clupper
Sandra Stone
Amy and Larry Zachery, and family
Rebecca Burns
Peter Lev
John Sorbo
Joanie Peacock
Barbara Relles
Laurel Healy
Greg Fairbrother
Phillip Fischer and Rosanne Solomon
Deborah Couzantino
Wilda Meier
Ken and Peggy Kaplan
Ardell Otten
Tom and Gail Myers
Zolla
David Ohlson

Nancy Janus
Celeste Currie
Jeff Lynn and Kitty Miller
Helene Robinson
Timi Hager
Dana Arace
Valerie B. Lipscomb
Richard and Janet King
Anthony Dalsimer
Susan E. Fulton
June Blaustein

Pat Coville
JoAnne Devries
Roger Fritts
Eugene Balis
Robin Danzak
Joanie Hazen
Carol Buchanan
Brendan Makowicz
Marilyn Nunan
Suzie Brucklacher
Bill Dalgarno

Index

Aboke girls *xxi*, *xxii*, 37, 45
Acan, Grace *xii*, *xxii*, 35, 73, 132
Aceng Okile, Emma *iii*, *iv*, *xii*, *xix*, *xx*, *xxii*, *xxiii*, 25, 46, 47, 57, 58, 60, 117, 118, 132
Acholi
    people 25
    sub-region 68
Action Fund (NUSAF) 65
Adiyo, Solomon 93, 95
adult education 49, 54
Akwang, Eunice *xii*, *xiii*, *xxii*, 60, 62, 63, 132, 137
Alternative to Violence Centred Organisation for Humanity (AVCOH) *xix*
Amuge Otengo, Rebecca 58
Banya, Kenneth 43
Barlonyo
    Early Childhood Development Centre 96
    massacre 12
Barlonyo Technical and Vocational Institute (BTVI) 83, 103
bride prices 131
charity work 70
child
    abductions *xvii*
    abuse *xxi*, 49, 115, 117, 120, 121
    labour 64, 115
    marriage(s), see early marriages 55, 141
    mortality 126, 131
    sacrifice 117, 120
    soldiers 29, 81, 92, 137
communal life 128
community
    connection (talk show) 118, 123
    dialogues 52, 79
    sharing 71
    transformation 124
community-based organisations (CBOs) 60, 62, 70
Concerned Parents Association (CPS) *xxi*, 35-39, 41, 43, 45
Convention on the Elimination of All Forms of Discrimination against Women (CEDAW) 52, 130
cooperative organisations 70
cross-cultural competence 71
Cross Cultural Foundation of Uganda (CCFU) 128
cultural
    capital 14
    development 127
    needs 70
development initiatives 128
domestic violence *xix*, *xxi*, 2, 3, 48, 49, 51, 52, 54, 57, 60, 68, 69, 79, 113, 114, 115, 117, 120, 121
early
    marriage(s) 28, 48, 81, 115
    pregnancy/ies 31, 50

economic dependency 69
Ekel, Margret *119*
Engola, Betty *60*
Engola, Sam *60*
Female Genital Mutilation (FGM) 13
gender
    abuse *117, 120*
    bias *57*
    equality *57, 96, 125, 131*
Gender Programme *118-120, 122, 123, 124, 142*
girl child *50, 51, 69, 114, 117*
girl's education *iii, 9, 50, 51, 56, 59, 69, 119*
HIV/AIDS *xix, 3, 29, 30, 31, 50, 55, 64, 65, 67, 117, 120, 123, 131, 136*
human
    development *117, 120*
    dignity *53*
    rights *xviii, 21, 52, 57, 122, 136*
income-generating activities *65, 66, 113, 115*
internally displaced persons (IDPS) *2*
International Women's Day *46, 101, 132, 142*
Justice and Reconciliation Project (JRP) *xxii, 73, 78, 141*
Karamojong cattle rustlers *26, 28*
Kony, Joseph *iii, iv, v, xvii, 1, 25, 32, 135, 137, 142*
land
    disputes *xxi, 49*
    wrangling *32*

Lango
    conference (2012) *33, 125*
    Cultural Foundation *127*
    culture *xxii, 127, 128*
    households *126*
    people/Langi *29, 53, 126, 127, 128*
    Region Development Agenda (LDA) *125*
    sub-region *iii, iv, xii, xviii, xx, xxi, 2, 25, 28, 30, 31, 32, 33, 34, 57, 59, 62, 81, 116, 119, 120, 122, 124-126, 131, 136*
life-devastating illnesses *131*
Lira community *xiii, xxv, 12*
loans schemes *71*
Local Defence Units (LDUs) *30*
Lord's Resistance Army (LRA) *xvii*
LRA insurgency *82*
mental health *xxiii, xxiv, 19, 21, 24, 137*
Millennium Development Goals (MDGs) *130*
Museveni Yoweri, Kaguta *54, 137*
Network (WAN) *xxii, 73*
non
    -agricultural products *71*
    -governmental organizations (NGOs) *51, 59*
Northern Uganda Social Action Fund (NUSAF) *65*
Ogwal, Consy *35, 36, 40, 74, 132*
Okwir, Regina Betty *iv, 60, 132*
Ongom, Joy *58*
post
    -traumatic growth *xxiv*
    -war challenges *6*
    -war poverty *32*

Post Traumatic Stress Disorders (PTSD) *34*
poverty eradication *51*
Psycho Aid International *119*
psychopathic behaviours *81*
psychosocial
  intervention *86*
  needs *124*
  recovery *82*
  services *xiii, 124*
  violence *52*
Rachele Comprehensive School *81, 91*
Rachele Rehabilitation Centre *81*
Rachele, Sister *xxi, xxiii, 36, 41, 43, 44, 81, 82, 91, 103, 104, 106, 141*
racial demarcation *22*
rebel
  -born children *81*
  soldiers *xvi, 2*
rehabilitation centre *81*
retrieval system *ii*
rural community *47, 48*
second-class citizens *3, 120*
self
  -esteem *60, 70, 87*
  -sustaining *3, 72*

Senyonga, Jackson *117*
sex slaves *xvii, 2*
sexual abuse *31, 50, 64*
spiritual beliefs *8*
story-telling project *79*
subsistence farming *81*
'Te-cwao' Youth and Elderly Association (TYEA) *x, 12, 62, 65*
therapeutic alliance *19*
Uganda National Culture Policy (2006) *128*
Uganda People's Defence Forces (UPDF) *xxi, 30*
Universal Primary Education (UPE) *49, 63, 80*
Universal Secondary Education (USE) *80*
vocational training *xxiv, 68, 82, 124, 137*
war-affected youth *94*
war-related psychological issues *124*
Women Achievers Group *xiii, 112, 113, 132*
Women's Advocacy *x, xxii, 71, 73, 78, 79*
women's empowerment *xxii*